MARCUS JAMIESON-POND

Hotel 1982

Discovering sex, cigars and rock and roll

For Diane, Harry and Millie.
Be grateful that I didn't know you then.

Also for my Dad.
Sorry you didn't get to read this nonsense.

Foreword

All of these events actually happened to one 18 year old West-Country boy in the early 80s.

Some of the details may have been lost over time and I concede that some of the conversations may have been embellished with a little artistic license.

The language and attitudes reflect the culture that existed. Thankfully wider society has become more tolerant of differences over the last 40 years and I hope that is the case in the hotel industry too.

For any parent thinking of giving their child advice about 'taking a gap year', read on.

Acknowledgement

Thanks to Nick Moses for the photograph, taken in 1983, and to all the people I met at the Hotel for giving me the education that every young person should have.

Additional thanks to my panel of review copy readers for their input: Tom; Michele & Niamh; Daniel; Sooz; Melanie and Jenny.

Thanks to Melanie for the idea to include Jimmy (Week 9).

Special thanks to Diane for her tolerance and proot reading skills.

HOTEL 1982

JUPITER HOTEL
YOUR MINI-BAR HAS BEEN CHECKED

Year Minus 1

My A-level results were pretty much as expected. Although that's not saying much. My results were what I was expecting, the school expected more and my parents hoped for a lot more than that. I think, with hindsight, my expectation management could have been better.

"They're not *that* bad", Mum had reassured me when I got home from picking up the envelope from school. But I could see she was thinking the opposite. I'd been lazy for two years and she had let me prioritise my social life over studying, but the fault was all entirely my own.

I'd been on a two year long academic roller coaster that came off the tracks in the exam hall. I knew that chemistry and physics were bad choices, mainly as I hadn't got a clue what was going on. But I had hoped that the hidden knowledge lurking inside my head would suddenly be recovered, or even discovered, when faced with an exam paper.

Unsurprisingly, it was never found - it wasn't there in the first place. Studying science, I should have known that miracles just don't happen, no matter how hard you pray for them. Being an atheist, I should have known that my prayers were pointless anyway.

Simply put, my sixth form had been spent either drunk, asleep, hung over, or in some stupor in between. Study time after school was substituted with hours wasted with my friends in The Gorge, a local cafe that had been lined with bright orange paper-mâché stalactites in an attempt to make it look like a cave.

The Gorge was in the middle of our provincial town, on the first floor of a shopping centre. I never knew if 'Gorge' was supposed to describe the decor, as in short for 'gorgeous'; was an instruction to 'gorge' yourself silly on stale cheese sandwiches; or was an oblique reference to Cheddar Gorge about 50 miles away. Either way, the coffee was grim, but the staff didn't seem to mind a group of school kids descending every weekday at 4 pm, or earlier if we were supposed to be in games lessons.

One cup of coffee + four (or more) teenagers = two hours sat at a dirty plastic laminated table talking shit about shit.

Something in my approach to school wasn't quite right. All homework time was reallocated to socialising. My weekday evenings were spent in The Gorge and my weekends disappeared at The New Lodge, which was one of two local pubs that seemed to actually encourage underage drinking. The New Lodge, which since changed its name to The *Old* Lodge, sits in the middle of a massive links golf course on top of a hill. It had a function hall which serviced the odd local band and became the go-to venue for every teenage party.

Nowadays The Old Lodge is a mid-price restaurant, frequented by aging duffers. The more things change they more they stay the same - today's respectable punters are probably the same group of people from the early 80s, who as teenagers used to stagger around outside, sick on booze, before sleeping

3

it off in the parked up golf carts.

It was a rite of passage to have an 18th Birthday party at The Lodge, and many 16th's took place there too - complete with cider on tap. The formula was simple - get pissed, do a bit of terrible dancing with the lads and then try to snog the face off your girlfriend, if you were lucky enough to have one. Or just look at the girls, in a slightly predatory way, if not.

All that happened to the sounds of Santana's 'She's not there'; Led Zep's 'Stairway to Heaven'; Clapton's 'Layla' and Lynyrd Skynyrd's 'Freebird'. If the blonde Danish DJ was feeling exotic, Third World's 'Now That We've Found Love' could make an appearance. There was a rumour that he had a Bob Marley album too, but I don't think it ever got an airing.

As a bribe, we'd offer him a pint of snakebite and black to play a 12 inch remix of something that would be a good backdrop for some serious kissing. He'd take the drink and play a series of three minute pop songs instead. Nobody wanted to snog to Abba's 'Waterloo', or the Birdy Song, and each time he was bought a pint, the music got even worse. He was serviced by a procession of free pints from lads requesting 'I Feel Love' or 'Sex Machine'. We lived in hope.

As I said, this was a provincial town and it liked its AOR/MOR. We were a community of soft rockers who thought bands like Yes, Rush, Genesis, Fleetwood Mac and Jethro Tull were trailblazers. There was no punk nor new wave for us yokels, even though The Jam had played a local gig when Paul Weller was apparently no more than ten years old. OK, maybe he was seventeen. I still have a memory of a poster on a public toilet wall, long demolished, advertising that event. I also remember laughing at my fourteen year old cousin who told me he was a punk. 'It'll never last. Have a listen to Mike Oldfield if you

4

want to hear some real music', I told him sagely.

The town that hosted the Jam gig was a good hour's walk away from The Lodge and much longer after four pints of 6X. Most of us lived there. Anyone who didn't get a lift home would be sober by the time they had staggered across the fairways, assuming that they didn't collapse in a bunker, or bump into one of the cows that were allowed to graze and leave cowpats on the fairways in the summer.

The fact that there wasn't anything, or anyone, within a mile's radius of the pub was probably why the police turned a blind eye to what went on. I suspect the remains of at least one wayward drunken teenager are still buried somewhere in a sand trap.

When we weren't 'up The Lodge', we'd be trying to gatecrash parties, or I'd be trying, and usually failing, to find places to get partially undressed with my girlfriend, Alison. We had met in our second term of sixth form and I had fallen deliriously in love with her, as you do if you've got an outstanding record of underachievement when it comes to chatting up girls. We would usually see each other every day before lessons, during lunch breaks and after school too. On getting home we'd spend at least an hour on the phone talking about nothing, other than how our parents wanted us to get off the line.

School had just become a way to get to see Alison and I found myself constantly drifting away from studies and gravitating towards day dreams about our future life together. The delusion of a love-sick obsessive youth is a powerful thing. You could probably run a 60 watt bulb off the energy that it

5

creates.

It would be fair to say that I had a pretty bad attitude to A-Level homework. Why waste good Alison telephone time on working out the different types of chemical bonds, learning equations involving mass and acceleration, or drawing pictures of zygotes? (Whatever those are). If only I had applied as much effort into studying as I did to making those phone calls and engineering opportunities for partying with her.

That social life kept me out most Friday and Saturday nights. It was funded in part by a Saturday morning milk round that I did in return for a beer voucher with the Queen's picture on it. As well as a fiver for 6 hours work, I was allowed to down a bottle of fizzy drink half way round the delivery route and was given as much buttered toast as I could eat back at the dairy. Sheer bloody luxury. The irony was that I didn't like the taste of milk, so the offers of a pint to 'keep you going' were always declined.

The milk round was a great way to learn my 17 times table (the price of a pint) and provided a free workout - I used to be able to lift 60 old style glass bottles full of milk from the floor to waist high. It's probably where my bad back came from, as well as a hatred of the gym. And no, milkmen don't get housewives inviting them in to warm up. Not this one anyway.

Sleep was for suckers (and straight A students). I'd be out until 2 am on Friday night, with Alison and the gang of lads from school and their girlfriends. This often went on way into the middle of the night, if my mate Simon came back to my house for coffee to discuss why his life was terrible. I'd be getting up before the sun at 5 am on a Saturday, still pissed, after two or three hours sleep to do the milk. This would be followed by more partying to 2 am on Saturday night/Sunday morning. No wonder I would be in bed for the rest of the weekend sleeping it off, sometimes with a bucket for company.

As the eldest son of four, I guess my parents had nothing to measure me against and took it as normal behaviour. My Mum still laughs about finding me semi-conscious in our garden at 2 am one night after I had tried, and failed, to 'do the gallon' of beer with Simon and a couple of other mates. They all had a much larger 'oil capacity' than I did and I think I gave up booze for a couple of weeks after that. I knew buying chips on the way home was a bad idea - those delicious hot potato slices had obviously poisoned me.

Homework would usually be done on Monday mornings before school, as long as I could find someone to copy it from. Obviously the transcription would have to include a few errors to put the teachers off the scent. I was only ever challenged for copying homework once and ironically that was for one of the rare pieces I had done myself. I responded with righteous indignation.

This way, for two years, I continued to remain slightly off the bottom of my classes and attributed mock exam results to nerves, even though on one multiple-choice paper the physics teacher pointed out that my score of 4% was statistically lower than had I just guessed, or answered option 'A' for every question. He wasn't reassured when I told him that my score meant I was 'nearly right' on 96% of the paper. I promised to answer 'A' for everything next time and settle for the theoretical 25% that would give me. I hated physics and it hated me.

There was a group of six or seven lads at the grammar school that I knocked about with. All of them were studying arts subjects and therefore were not the spods that offered me their science homework on Monday mornings. My mates didn't realise how badly I was doing and I wish one of them had shaken me up and told me to get a grip before it was too late. But I could move between the science geeks and my fey friends with self-delusional ease. After all, I was doing O Levels in Art and Economics & Public Affairs in my spare time, for fun. If I had time to get B grades in those, then surely I understood the basics of valency and differentiation, or so my friends would tell me, on the way to buy another pint.

I was envious of those of my school friends that got to read books rather than having to play with test tubes and getting their minds fucked trying to calculate the area under a graph. I'd much rather had been lounging in a library like Wilde in a dressing gown, than perching on a stool in a white lab coat with my latest chemistry practical disaster in front of me. I didn't discover anything new in chemistry, nor in physics, other than I sucked at both subjects equally. I often wondered why had I followed my brain rather than my heart when choosing my A level subjects. My heart was pretty much located in the girls' school next door for most of the sixth form anyway.

————

Of all of the group of literary students, Richard and I were besties. I had a great deal of time for him, to the point that I pretty much lived in his shadow...and I was more than happy to lurk there. He was cool and by attaching myself like a limpet, I must have thought I would be ice cold by association.

Richard was half French and had long dark curly hair. He had an air of supreme self-confidence, to the point of arrogance, and played guitar better than anyone I knew. The first time

I heard Jimi Hendrix I was sat in his bedroom and the first time a NASA shuttle was launched, I watched the blast-off sat in his lounge. Of the two events, I suspect Hendrix made the more lasting impact. I didn't rush out and purchase all of Neil Armstrong's back catalogue from the local second-hand record shop when Columbia went into space.

Where Richard led, I followed. After he had played me that first Hendrix album ('Rainbow Bridge'), I bought up everything I could find on vinyl - including some of the earlier, more shitter, stuff that still gets rehashed as LPs of 'rare tracks'. To this day I still have a gap on the shelf where the Rainbow Bridge Original Soundtrack should be - perhaps that shows a degree of unconscious homage to that period of my history. Or maybe I just haven't found a copy in a second-hand shop since. Either way, I think it is fair to say that I had developed a man/boy crush on Jimi, as well as Richard.

It wasn't long before I was wearing a matching navy trench coat, collarless shirt and similar Kickers desert boots. That's similar to Richard's, not Jimi's, obviously. Jimi's wardrobe was way cooler than that. I'm sure casual observers would probably have said I was copying Richard to the point of trying to be him. Mimicry is said to be the greatest form of flattery, even if it may have made Rich and I look like twinny twins.

———

Within our gang we were the dos amigos. Our friends knew us as two of the lads who put on early raves in local village halls - our third leg being Simon, who was the school's only A Level Art student and had access to the printing press the art department kept in a locked room. He would do us some posters and tickets 'under the counter' when the teachers weren't about.

The three of us had decided it was time to stop being the wallflowers we had grown into during the 5th form. 6th form was going to be our time to get noticed. We just needed a way to be the centre of attention. We could be heroes, just for one day, or for longer if we played our cards right.

So we hit upon the idea to hire old crusty rooms in village halls for an evening, at a cost of about £15. A DJ mate in the year above us (the same one who took the beer bribes at The New Lodge) would do us a disco for £20 and a couple of snakebite and blacks and we'd charge our fellow schoolmates 75p for an entry ticket, on the promise of some free booze and a boogie.

We thought that was a way of getting around licensing laws. We'd simply be giving cans of Eastern European lager to under-aged drinkers, who were attending our paid-for party. They weren't buying booze and we weren't selling it - our 'guests' were just purchasing tickets to get in and helping themselves to the cans of dubious liquid found in a corner of the hall. Fortunately the theory was never tested by the police.

Those nights were based on the New Lodge formula - booze, embarrassing dancing and snogging. Despite living in the country, pretty much nobody did drugs, not even weed. This was well before raves went mainstream and needed chemical accompaniment to keep punters on the dance floor all night. Our parties were less Summer of Love and more Springtime of Lust.

As we were too young to buy alcohol, we had to rely on a parent who had recently split from his wife to get us stocked up. He was desperate to do anything to keep his kids on his side and keep custody. We'd ask his son Danny, our classmate, to procure a few crates for us via his paranoid father. Lucky for us, Danny's dad was happy to turn our 75ps into cans and bottles. 'Anything cheap with a high alcohol content, and a lot of it', was always the brief. Danny's dad would deliver it to the venue in his clapped out green 2CV as well.

Even with Danny's best efforts we never had enough booze (partly as his dad had a habit of buying Party Six kegs and we had no way of opening them). So the events tended to get a bit aggie with youths demanding their money's worth. There is nothing worse than trying to open a big tin of beer with a biro and a pebble whilst a baying mob is shouting in your ear. Especially if all you really want to do was find a dark corner for dirty deeds.

By midnight we would inevitably end up hiding from half pissed classmates and were grateful for the police when they would show up to relay neighbourly complaints about noise. It gave us the perfect reason to shut the thing down. 'Blame the police', 'Blame the neighbours', 'Blame Thatcher', but don't blame us. Refund? Come off it mate. Read the non-existent ts&cs.

Without fail, we would lose our damage deposits due to the 'disgusting mess' that had been left, or worse. At one party we had to close the event early when 6 or 7 dancing lads went through the floor. Fortunately no one was hurt. They just ended up a couple of feet below, coming to rest on top of the cellar ceiling, rather than disappearing into the depths. The Jam's 'Going Underground' was on when the floor gave way. You couldn't make it up - I didn't think anyone would take it as an instruction.

Danny had been brought in as a full organising partner for that particular party (mainly as a way to secure the booze supply line). The morning after the rave, Richard, Simon,

Danny and I met up at the old Cotswold stone venue half way up a hill, to talk to the Chair of the Village Hall Committee, who was demanding that we paid to have the floor replaced. To be fair to her, it did look a lot worse in daylight than it had done the night before. I was half expecting a sniper's head to pop out of one of the newly formed fox holes.

She was demanding £600 from the four of us in compensation. We made less than £20 a week in pocket money between us, if we were lucky, so any repayment plan would be a lifelong burden. For some reason, Danny's dad then appeared and agreed that the demands were reasonable and so we ended up having to have an argument with him, rather than the owner of the hall. Talk about putting up a united front.

After much point making by Richard and myself to both Danny's treacherous dad and the Village Hall Committee woman, the hall manager/caretaker showed up and accepted that the floor wasn't designed for dancing and we shouldn't have been allowed to book the space. We were supposed to be in the room upstairs, but that had been closed for redecoration. He accepted that we had told him there would be a disco and he should have turned us away.

Given that revelation, we walked out without making any payment (although I suspect Danny's dad slipped them some cash). I think that was my first brush with the law of tort and the concept of event insurance, as well as fine print in contracts. I also learned how to lay wooden floor tiles - joints on the beams, not in between.

Following that tricky situation, Simon and Danny both opted out of future organising roles, quitting in the Village Hall car park before going home. Richard and I put it down to not having the stomach for future fights with local council officials. But it did mean that we would have to find a new way of printing tickets and accessing booze, neither of which had an obvious solution. Danny's dad had retired along with his son and Simon was the only student the school trusted enough to be allowed near the art department's printing press. Little did they know what he was doing with it.

I suspected that there had also been an all-points bulletin put out around the Parish Council meetings to look out for devilish grammar school oiks intent on causing havoc. 'Beware those who would inflict pain and suffering upon your church halls, for they are not meek and mild, but will make your floor most holy'.

We had run out of village halls that would host our 'quiet parties for a few people' and had lost our alcohol supplier.

Conclusion 1: No venue + no booze = not much chance of selling tickets.

Conclusion 2: The party was over.

The broken floor had broken the partnership, but we didn't need to organise more parties anyway. We had cracked the social circle and hit our primary objective.

We had run the parties to become famous in our own lunchtimes and didn't expect to make money from them. However, even with all the damage and other costs, we managed to make the best part of £100 profit from each event. Doing the sums it would suggest that we definitely didn't worry about breaking the fire limits on numbers of attendees and were habitually ignoring health and safety regulations. Either that, or we bought a lot less booze than I remember.

At least I can look back on those times in 1980/81 and say that I used to run 'raves' before the word was invented. I was a 17 year old event planner with attitude, an impresario of sorts.

Talk about cool factor plus 10. Richard and I were climbing up the social ladder, two rungs at a time.

— — — —

Those dubious drunken events had the side benefit of making us social magnets. There was nothing better than selling tickets to the girls in the lane outside school, or turning down the hard lads when they wanted to make a block booking. We were the gatekeepers to dance heaven and the boys who had given us a hard time in the playground a couple of years back, when they thought we were nobodies, were never going to get through our pearly gates. Call it divine retribution. Your name's not down so you're not coming in, you greebo Garni*.

Richard and I used our elevated status to try to get invited back to other people's parties. We would often turn up at those that we didn't get invites to and attempt to talk our way in. With hindsight, that was a pretty shitty thing to do to someone who obviously didn't want us there in the first place. Invariably those evenings would end up being spent on a village square's memorial bench sharing a can of Castlemaine 4X and admiring the views across a random valley, whilst reassuring each other that the party was 'probably crap' anyway.

Luckily for everyone, after a couple of months and a couple of raves, we no longer had to crash house parties, or sneak past security at The Lodge. ('Security' being the unfortunate parent of the kid who was having a birthday party).

Richard and I had finally and firmly become established as part of the group of cool kids that met in the Common Room that was shared between the boys' and the girls' school 6th forms. We had created our clique (or maybe had broken into

14

someone else's) and would hang out there at break times to offer advice to both lads and girls in need of a shoulder to cry on.

Richard was King Louie holding court, and I'd be sat in a corner looking more like a lanky Baloo the Bear, with Alison perched on my skinny knees. I was known for organising great parties and was labeled a 'good listener' by the girls from the High School, and eventually that had become attractive enough for a girl to say yes to a date. And, lucky for me, she was the most attractive girl in the year too. How we got together, God only knows.

My top tip to any spotty lad who is suffering from social awkwardness and who wants to get a girlfriend is still to hire a hall, book a DJ and flog some tickets. Then go round the hall saying 'I did this, can I have your number?' Instant hero power.

Rich and I had gone from two shy lads in the fifth form to the centre of the social circle in less than six months. Girls wanted to talk to us and our introverted student mates came out of their cocoons to flit as multi-coloured butterflies in our wake. Even the uber-shy Simon was dragged out of his chrysalis of self-doubt, although he developed the rep as the lad who always turned to booze to create a comfort zone. There has to be one of those in every year group. Maybe he had an undiagnosed allergy to alcohol, or maybe he was just a piss-head.

———

Our evolution was quite an achievement and really got on the nerves of the thugs in the year – those from the moth-riddled Forest of Dean and some that lived in caves near Gloucester. One of our joint claims to fame was both our names appearing on the Common Room wall under a heading 'People we will kill before we leave school'. I was only ranked at 5th but Richard was where he always wanted to be - Number 1, with a bullet. The rest of the chart was made up with those lads who we would drink with on a regular basis and who would attend the court of King Richie at break times.

We guessed who had constructed the felt tip pen list - the hard-knocks that we had turned away from our raves. The same ones that always wanted to play Black Sabbath and AC/DC on the cassette player we had borrowed from the music room. Those lads only had two subjects of conversation: motorbikes, even though none of them owned one, and cider. These were the real yokels, those who lived near 'the River' in 'the Forest' and got the school bus from Frampton, wherever that is.

There was a lot of speculation that the people from the Forest were all related to each other and the gene pool wasn't that strong as a result. Cider and heavy metal seemed to prove that, as well as the fact that without fail they all had one of five surnames. There was more than one boy in our year who was another boy's uncle, as well as his brother.

Mr Young, our Head of Year, invited those of us who had appeared on the Top 10 into his office and asked us if we were upset about the graffiti. He asked if we knew who had composed the chart. We said we had no idea. Secretly, we thought of being on an assassin's hit-list as a badge of honour, but told him that we were worried about being attacked in the toilets by lads wearing steel toe-capped boots straight from their dads' building sites. We couldn't reveal the authors' names, for fear of retribution. But Mr Young probably worked out that the meatheads who had chosen A Level metalwork as an option, and had been suspended for making Ninja Stars during lessons, could well have been responsible.

Of course death never happened to anyone on the list, as bullies find it a lot easier to execute threats than perform the executions themselves. The closest we got to being killed by a meathead in a mullet was a bit of jostling in the lunch queue and having the odd bit of 'gob' spat in our general direction. Mind you, I did cross the road a few times when I saw more than one of that gang coming towards me. They all seemed to have this weird way of walking - knees pointing outwards, striding bow-legged with their hands deep in their bell-bottomed trouser pockets. It was either a sign of having spent too much time on imaginary motorbikes or, more likely, having sore gonads from enjoying too many hand shandies.

— — — —

School was over and the hard lads had failed in their ambition to enact ten executions. We had our Summer of Booze, waiting for our exam results to come out, and I spent at least a couple of weeks feeling really sorry for myself when they did. All of my mates got what they needed to get into the courses they wanted. They were heading to Uni, Alison was on her way to Leeds and I would be going into Clearing without much hope of picking up a course I really wanted to do with my 'Two Bs, one E and an O'. (I had managed to be awarded a second O-Level in Physics, which was quite an achievement after two years copying homework on Monday mornings. At least it wasn't an F).

It transpired that my friends were, without a shadow of a doubt, a lot more intelligent than I was and I shouldn't have believed them when they told me that they 'hadn't done the homework'. It turned out, I was the only one who hadn't bothered, relying on an unnatural talent that I didn't actually possess. Hoping for good grades and working for them were two entirely different things it seemed.

I thought it was possible to learn the laws of physics through osmosis (after all I was good at biology) and that chemistry was something to be found in a conversation at a party, rather than in a lab coat and dripping a liquid through a pipette. I was a bad student. I knew sciences weren't for me when I chose them, but I had always had a passion for biology and thought the only way to go on to do a degree in that subject would be to combine it with chemistry and physics. Only I didn't have a clue what was going on in those lessons and had too much pride to put my hand up to ask.

My 12 O levels (13 if you count the second one in physics) didn't seem to count for anything and the grade B in General Studies A level, that I'd taken the year before, wasn't looked at seriously by University admissions people. It was a six hour general knowledge test that would only be useful if I was applying to go on Mastermind.

September arrived and I was left alone at home. My mates were gone, and Alison, my girlfriend of 1 year, 10 months, 26 days and 4 hours, had departed to some big city in Yorkshire. I had no reason to go to the pub anymore and there would be no more parties ending in a fumble in the back of her black Cortina Estate, which my mates nicknamed 'The Hearse'. Those deep conversations about what we would do together in the future seemed lost in time. All I had left were a few photos and a lot of pens and paper, which I used to draft soppy poems and write the most bleak and deadly depressing letters that any girl could hope to receive.

It's no wonder that so many school relationships break up shortly after university term starts. What girl wants to have an anchor dragging them back home to a life long forgotten? I imagined her new found friends saying, 'Your boyfriend must really love you - he writes so many letters.' Little did I know that with each letter I was sealing my reputation as the Emperor of the Embarrassing Twats.

For the first time in my life I was really miserable, as opposed to just a bit depressed. Mr Young suggested I came back to school to resit my mediocre exams. I had been useless before, why would I be any better this time? I told him. And I would be in my younger brother's year too. Could I adapt to that humiliation? No. Another year at school just wasn't an option.

I was offered the chance to take the exams at Christmas instead, without the need to do lessons. I thought about the idea of home study for about two minutes and realised that would be futile. I could barely get out of bed before mid-afternoon, and the idea of getting up for physics and chemistry revision made me want to hibernate even more. I wasn't sure how chemistry practicals would work in my parents' shed either. Apparently I would be allowed to go into the labs for those and even do sessions on my own if I was too embarrassed. Rather than embarrassed I just felt like an abject failure and didn't really appreciate that the school was trying to help me out of compassion, rather than the guilt I thought it was at the time. My inability to get my grades was 100% down to me and not poor teaching. 'How could you have allowed me to copy other kids' homework?' seemed a bit of a poor defence for the predicament I found myself in.

I decided that I would look at other ways to get onto a degree course and take a gap year whilst sorting that out. How difficult

could it be? I'd travel, work and build up my CV, so that I could take those experiences forward with me through life. All I needed now was a plan, an offer of a place on a course for the following Autumn and a McJob to keep me out of trouble.

If the degree applications didn't work out, perhaps I could stumble into a Plan B and find something meaningful to do. After all, some of the lads who left after fifth form were now Junior Assistants to the Assistant Branch Manager at the local Barclays. Two years ago, I thought of them as too thick to do A-Levels, now they were wearing suits down the pub, buying more than two drinks and talking about mortgages and getting married. One even drove his own car to work.

I was moping about. My Mum was worried about me. She could see I had lost any zing I may have had before results day. She kept reassuring me that, 'Something will come up.'

My Dad tried to offer me careers advice and even found me a job in his factory sweeping up swarf. It was the lowest of the lowest jobs, working around the milling machines, clearing up metal shards. I didn't take it. I was too proud. In less than a couple of weeks, I had gone from having dreams of starting at Reading Uni to do my BSc Biology degree, to being offered a menial occupation at a factory making bits for oil rigs. I told him I had other things to do. I just had to find them now so that I could avoid getting sucked into the machine room. Plan B definitely did not involve a lathe or anything resembling a broom.

———

'Come to London', Richard had written on the back of a postcard that arrived in late September 1982. That would give me something to keep me occupied for a weekend and keep my Dad off my back for a couple of days. My tactic of spending most of the day in bed and most of the night playing early video games on a ZX Spectrum, instead of looking for work, was beginning to wear a bit thin. If that sounds depressing, it really was.

Rich had been in London since the Summer and was the only one of our gang who was taking a planned year out. London and Richard seemed like a good distraction and I was sure my Mum would be glad to have a break from seeing my miserable face.

So, with an emergency £10 note that Mum had slipped me on my way out to the bus, along with a spare pair of pants, a toothbrush and obligatory Penguin Classic in my army surplus knapsack, I strolled on to the platform and watched the blue and yellow High Speed Train roll in. Not so long ago I would have been excited by the 253 number on the front under the driver's windscreen, now I was just happy to get the hell outta Dodge.

— — — —

*Garni - This had nothing to do with flavouring. Local legend had it that there was a large family who lived out towards the River that had the reputation for committing petty mis-demeanours, burglary and theft. Any act of criminality would usually be blamed on the Garni clan. I am to this day unsure if the Garnis actually existed, or if they were just the local bogeyman, dreamt up to take the blame for any crime the police couldn't solve. Anyway, the term 'Garni' became used by all kids in the area to describe someone who was a bit unsavoury. 'Chav' is probably a good modern day translation.

I made the mistake of thinking that 'Garni' was in common English use and was often confronted by puzzled faces when describing dodgy people as being 'a right Garni' (in a strong Gloucestershire accent), when I was living in Oxford in my 20s.

Day Minus 1

I had arranged a weekend trip down to London to see my amigo, the other half of the Dude Twins.

Richard was renting a room in West Hampstead from one of his older brother's dons. The brother, Charles, had 'gone up' to Oxford Uni the year before. Despite his obvious raw intellect he would soon be close to going back down, after throwing a breeze-block through the windscreen of a car belonging to his tutor, as you do when your intelligence is questioned. I could stay with Richard at his digs and go out to see the sights. It seemed a more agreeable plan than spending a weekend avoiding another conversation with my Dad about sweeping the factory floor.

I arrived at midday on the Friday. The train pulled into Paddington and people started to disembark. Richard was stood on the platform waiting for me.

"Good to see you bro", he said, his dark curly hair bouncing up and down as he jogged up in the opposite direction to the passengers, nearly knocking a couple over.

He stood there in front of me and I realised that we were both wearing our second-hand charity shop uniform - brown cord jackets, collarless granddad shirts and Kicker boots. We looked like a couple of rejects from a really really bad boy band, or a Wurzels tribute act. I made a mental note, 'Time to stop copying his dress code'. I had bought the same shit clothes as Richard for the last two years and maybe now I needed to find my own style, for both our sakes.

"Look at what I found for you", Richard exclaimed, excitedly pointing at the Evening Standard newspaper he was clutching like a medieval play sword. A newspaper? Big wow.

Before we got to the end of the platform, he opened the paper to the classified jobs and showed me the entry that he had circled whilst waiting for the train to arrive. 'Central London Hotel requires mini-bar attendant.' Being more than six feet tall, I was confused. *(Badoom-ching, I'm here all week folks!)*

"It's what I'm doing in Hyde Park!" Richard informed me. But I was still none the wiser.

"Posh hotels have fridges in them full of little bottles of booze that the guests can knock back if they can't be arsed to go to the bar. I've got a job filling them up. It's the fucking easiest way to make money in this town."

And?

"Apply for this job. It might be at my hotel too, so how cool would that be? You can move to London and we can both be mini-bar attendants."

I don't think so. After all I was only coming for the weekend and only had the emergency clothing that my Mum had made me take with me as I left the house a couple of hours earlier. I wasn't prepared for anything other than short haul.

"You've got no choice man. Here's 10p to make the call. If you don't call them, you can fuck off back to the country. I don't do visitors, unless they are called Harriet and want to sleep with me. And by the way, if they ask if you're a student, or planning to go to Uni, say no."

On the platform concourse a bank of payphones greeted me. 'Welcome to London, your new life starts here' read a large sign above them. OK, what the hell, be brave, give them a call and Richard will get off my back. At the very least I'll be able to grab some lunch before he sends me home with my tail between my legs.

"Come in for an interview, bring your resume." Was the reply when I got through to the Staff Department, "Shall we say 2 pm?"

What the actual fuck? How was I going to explain what I looked like? I wasn't dressed to impress and didn't have a CV with me. In fact, I didn't own one. Spontaneous interviews were not something we had been told about during the one careers lesson we were dragged through back in school. But Richard was chuffed.

"Welcome to London indeed my friend. Which hotel was it?"

The Jupiter, on Grosvenor Square, apparently quite close to Bond Street tube station. I guess we better make our way down there.

— — — —

We found the five star 1920's red brick hotel on the outskirts of Mayfair. A huge Union Jack and a blue European Union flag fluttered outside in the autumnal breeze. I realised that I had never actually been into a proper hotel before, not even a one star version.

The dude on the door, who I later discovered was called a concierge, was dressed in a gray tail coat and sported a green top hat. He eyed me up and down suspiciously.

"Can I help you?" he inquired, with the subtext of 'who, what and why on earth' left hanging in the atmosphere between us. I told him I was there for an interview and he quickly ushered me though the heavy glass doors and across the hotel lobby to the top of a staircase, which looked as if it may have led to the fire exit. I thought for a moment I would find myself outside if I went through the door in front of me.

"Go downstairs. You need to ask for the Staff Department and they'll take care of you."

Five minutes later I was sat in a cramped underground office, which was lined with wobbly shelving, housing what I presumed were the contents of the staff records in battered box-files.

In front of me across the desk, my interviewer, a sharp suited man in his 30s, offered me a cigarette, which I declined, before lighting up one of his own.

"Do you have a CV?"

I had to confess that I didn't. I didn't own one, but thought it better to explain that three hours before I hadn't had a clue that I was going to be doing this today. I told him that I had seen his advert in the Standard, given the hotel a call and here I was. I also apologised for looking like a hippy. Because I didn't know I was going to have an interview, I told him all my suits were at home. Of course, I didn't actually own a suit, unless a redundant school uniform counted.

"Are you planning to go to University?"

"No. I'm hoping to make a career in hotels. Who knows maybe one day I may even end up being the manager of this place." I offered in reply.

"I don't think so. Have you ever worked in hotels before?"

"No. But I did do a paper round and then a milk round, when I was at school. I appreciate that may not be the same as what

26

you want me to do here, but I am used to working rubbish hours and handling bottles of stuff. Although I understand we are talking about small bottles of booze, rather than pints of milk. Oh and doing the milk was good for developing customer service skills. Not that anyone was awake that early in the morning." He smiled. It looked like I had cracked it.

"OK. Can you start the day after tomorrow? The pay is £2 per hour and you will be working a 40-hour week. Two other things. A piece of advice - don't go to any job interviews wearing Kickers again and get a haircut before you come back."

— — — —

Twenty minutes later.

"Hi Mum. This may sound a bit strange, but I'm not coming home on Sunday after all. Richard has persuaded me to stay in London. I'm going to be starting a job in a West End hotel, in the mini-bar department. Damn, that's the pips and I don't have any more change. I'll call you after I've finished work on Sunday."

"Time for a celebratory meal, good buddy", Richard enthused. Let's go for a walk along Oxford Street and find somewhere. Do you know Angus Steakhouse? Maybe that's a bit expensive. Or there's a McDonald's at the end near Marble Arch tube. Tell you what, I shall show you the cheapest way to eat in London instead. Follow me."

So I followed Richard straight into the nearest Garfunkels, a shiny pizza/pasta joint. Impressively egalitarian, with just a whiff of Italy about it, not that I had ever been on a aeroplane before, let alone to Italy. The closest I had been to that country was probably collecting Panini stickers of their national

27

football team, but I recognised pizza and pasta when I saw it.

"Now. What we do here is genius. Look and learn my friend. Look and learn. All the hustle with none of the hassle."

The waitress came over to the table and Richard placed our order.

"Can we have the salad plate, but with two plates please. So that's one plate and an extra plate." And to me, "You OK with water, or do you want to go mad and have a coke?" I shrugged.

Richard went back to the bemused waitress, "That'll be one large coke with two straws and no ice please." He explained that ice was just frozen water and we could get that for free from a tap. "Never ever order ice, especially not in a foreign restaurant," was his advice. I wondered if Garfunkels counted as 'foreign'.

Richard took the plate, but not the extra plate, to the salad bar and built a monumental construction of various leaves and round objects, bound together with sauces of different colours and descriptions. I watched and learned his useful life lesson.

"You have to get the balance right. Start with a foundation of lettuce leaves. They have strong spines and you can hang them over the edge of the plate like this. Straight away your plate is nearly doubled in diameter and it means there's more space to load other stuff on."

He put the plate down next to the tanks of various food products, most of which appeared to be contaminated with beetroot.

"I then go with garlic bread. Put a couple of layers of that around the edge of the plate, on top of the lettuce, making a sort of outer castle wall. We can load up the edges of the lettuce sticking out from under the wall later on with the likes of sweet corn, or anchovies. Anything light enough to sit on the leaves,

28

but not heavy enough, or round enough, to fall off on the way back to the table."

"We then start to fill the castle with anything you fancy. I'd go small tomatoes, coleslaw, stacks of tuna and ham – we need our protein and that's also the expensive stuff. This is an exercise in getting our money's worth after all. Croutons?" I nodded, although they looked more like bread crumbs to me.

"Let's have some of this stuff too – not sure what it is. It's green and smells of vinegar, so it must be OK."

"Et voila! We have our salad and the cheapest meal in London."

Once the mountain of food had been transported to the table, about a third was decanted off onto the extra plate.

"Having fun boys?" the waitress enquired flatly when delivering our singular glass of coke. She'd seen it all before. And it was probably Richard who starred in those prequels.

It was enough food to feed maybe four or five strapping mini-bar attendants and given that this was mid-afternoon, I suspected it would be my final meal of the day, unless Richard had another cunning plan. He had obviously developed a nose for sniffing out cheap food since he had been in London. It was Richard who had introduced me to my first kebab, bought in a takeaway on Tottenham Court Road when we had made a trip to London to look at guitar shops when we were in the 4th form and he had joined a band. That was a bargain too and the most exotic thing I had ever tasted.

————

A few years later I would recreate the Garfunkels plate trick to try to impress a girlfriend. Only that time, the lettuce failed to support the garlic bread and most of the contents ended up on the floor on the way back to the table. When the bill arrived, I questioned why we had been charged for two meals, when only one of us had been to the salad bar.

"Two plates equals two meals." Was the reply from a less than impressed manager. "We charge by the plate, so pay up or do the washing up." Garfunkels had obviously had too many visits from Richard in the intervening period. Ah well, there goes the rest of my money for two pints of beer and a tube home, I thought. Let's just hope she isn't thirsty and doesn't mind walking. Ever the gent.

— — — —

The day was coming together nicely. I had the job and had witnessed food robbery at first hand. I now needed some sort of black trousers, white shirt and black shoes, that would make up my side of the uniform. The hotel would supply a jacket and bow tie.

"I know just the place on top of Oxford Circus tube," Richard assured me. "It's called Mr Byrite. They sell all manner of cheap shit there. And as your Barclaycard only has a £100 limit on it, you will need the cheapest shit going." I wondered how he knew about my credit limit.

Mr Byrite, or Mr By-RI-tee as I thought it must be pronounced, was suitably stacked with the cheapest of cheap clothing. The type that would probably ignite if worn on a warm Summer's day. I didn't know about the reaction between man-made fibres and sweaty worker bodies at that point - indeed, the closest I had got to antiperspirant was watery deodorant flavoured with what smelt like car air freshener. But that didn't stop me loading up with two white 15 inch collar polyester shirts, just like the ones from school, and a pair of black trousers, 32 inch waist. OK, the legs didn't reach my ankles, but they came at a bargain price that ended in .99 so I could live with that.

I had never really been proper clothes shopping before. So I decided to keep it real in the bargain buckets. Actually, I had no choice and yet had still spent half a week's wages on half of a uniform before I had even started work. There was no going back now, well not until I had earned enough cash to pay off the balance on my credit card.

Shoes next. At that time, every other shop on Oxford Street was a shoe shop (before they were converted into tatty souvenir emporia). I soon found a pair of black shoes that 'would do', although of course I would soon discover that they really wouldn't do for an 8 hour shift and a young man with sweaty feet. Satan's Trousers? Satan's brogues more like. I'd spray them with Lynx, but they would still stink, only now a little more exotically. Those shoes would end up sitting on the windowsill over night, every night, in an attempt to let the stench out. I hoped that someone who had lost their sense of smell would take them to justify me buying a less synthetic pair. However, every morning, without fail, they would be there, damply waiting and the dance of the fetid feet would start again.

Richard and I hopped on the tube and headed up the relatively new Jubilee line to West Hampstead where he was living. He told me I could kip on the woefully small sofa for the night and try to find somewhere more permanent to live whilst he was at work the next day. No pressure then.

Mr Biddle, his landlord, was obviously a highly educated

and learned fellow. His rooms were lined with books about ancient people, lost civilizations and objects of uncertain origin. He peered over his half-framed glasses from his ripped red leather Chesterfield chair, as Richard introduced me as his friend from the country. Mr Biddle replied, "Of course you are" and returned to his book. No sign of a smile. A man of little emotion, he obviously preferred reading words than using them.

Richard lent over to flick a switch on the stereo amplifier and asked me to pass him a copy of Steely Dan's 'Can't Buy a Thrill', which was next to the record deck. "This is cool" he told me. I already knew that, the record had been on the decks at most of our friends' houses for the last year.

The vinyl started to make a small scratching sound, but beyond that nothing. I suggested he needed to turn the volume up, but I was rebuked.

"Come on," said Richard, "We'll listen to it downstairs. That's the cool bit." The house was wired up with two sets of speakers – one in Mr Biddle's study and the other in the kitchen, down in the basement. That really was the coolest thing I had ever seen.

We sat at a long kitchen island in a very designer black marble and white laminate-doored kitchen as 'Do It Again' played from hidden speakers. The kitchen was such a contrast to the one at home, which sported a single fluorescent tube. Mr Biddle's subterranean cooking bunker had light from every angle – uplighters, downlighters, some as big as your head. I wondered what if my Mum's food would taste better if I could see it.

"Right. What's for dinner? You hungry? Looks like we're low on options. Buddle can't have been shopping today", Richard said, leaning into the fridge. "What a bastard. How am I supposed to steal his food if he hasn't got any?"

'In the morning you go gunning for the man who stole your water' – sang Steely Dan. I wondered if Mr Biddle would be gunning for Richard in the morning, even though water came out of taps for free.

"Chips?" Richard brushed the ice off a plastic bag from the freezer and turned the grill on. We were living the high life alright. Grilled chips? They filled a gap, as did the couple of beers that Richard found hidden in a bread bin. We talked some more about nothing in particular and continued to search and liberate the odd bit of food from the cupboards. Richard was certainly still King Louie and was glad of an appreciative audience.

What a day. Here I was. My first night in the big city, feeling slightly sick on a sofa with just my coat to cover me for warmth and a bag of Mr Byrite basics to keep me company. Welcome to London.

Day 0

T he next day Richard woke me at 7 am to tell me he was off to his hotel on Hyde Park Corner to fill some mini-bars. He wished me good luck in my search for somewhere to live.

I was a new boy in town, without a clue where to find a temporary home. I'd never been flat hunting and wasn't really sure how to start. I wandered up to the parade of shops next to West Hampstead tube station and found a greasy spoon cafe to get some breakfast.

On my way, I had looked at lettings in a couple of estate agents windows. West Hampstead was definitely out of my price range. I realised that I would not be shopping for private two bed flats and the best, affordable, option would be a lot less glamorous. I would probably need to narrow down the search to look for a room in a shared house, hopefully with something more than a sofa to sleep on.

"Get a place in Zone 1 or 2" Richard had advised me. "And if it's near to me then all the better, at least you won't have to walk far if you want a cup of Buddle's tea." He had drawn a circle in the A to Z map book I had bought in the WHSmith at Paddington the day before and that was going to be my search area for the day.

The plate of scrambled eggs on toast slid down nicely. Richard had told me that the main train stations got their copies of the Evening Standard ahead of everywhere else, so in much the same way that I had been ahead of the curve by looking at jobs when I had arrived at Paddington, I could do the same with accommodation.

Given that I knew where it was, I hoped onto the tube and headed back down to Paddington. It wasn't the closest station, but the one I was most familiar with and there would always be trains there ready to take me back to the West Country if I lost my nerve.

I stood waiting by a news stand just outside the main entrance, watching the stream of black cabs going in and out, bringing in a spate of passengers and taking new arrivals to who knows where in town. I wondered if I would ever have enough money in my pocket to be able to shout TAXI at a passing cab and ask them to take me to an exotic location filled with life changing experiences.

The papers arrived. I paid my few pence and opened it at the accommodation pages. All I had to do was find a flat, bedsit, or more likely a shared room in a house that I could just about afford - maybe about £100 a month tops and make sure it was within walking distance of Richard's place. A new city without any local mates would be a very unfriendly and hostile environment otherwise.

Applying my budget and Richard's target circle over most of North West London, only three classified adverts made the cut. I returned to the bank of phones I had been at 24 hours earlier and took out the pile of 10p pieces that Richard had offered me in exchange for a couple of £1 notes.

The phone at advert one was answered by a horse sounding

man with a heavy accent. "No, we only want girls here." He said when I asked him if the room was still free. His phone clicked. I thought, "Hey at least he was being honest." Then I thought, "Why only girls?" Two to go.

Advert two seemed more promising. "Yes it is a shared house in Kilburn. You come now I can show you. £140 a month plus bills." Price wise it was more than I had expected, but I thought maybe it would be worth it and I could always try to economise elsewhere. The landlord told me where the house was in Kilburn, and suggested I made the short journey over there as soon as possible, as he expected the first person who came would take it.

I jumped on the Circle line and after a change at Baker St, got out at Kilburn tube. The area seemed very run down compared to West Hampstead, but it was a slice of real London life. As long as I wasn't likely to get mugged, it would be OK.

It turned out that the house was a short walk from the tube station. Promising. And the station was in Zone 2, even better.

The semi-detached Victorian building definitely needed some cosmetic tender loving care on the outside. A couple of buddleia plants had found a foothold in the bottom stone step leading up to the front door, which in turn was missing a pane of stained glass that had been replaced by a piece of old weathered chipboard, that looked like it had been there a while. The house had been painted at some point in the last 100 years too. Closer to 1892 than to yesterday I thought.

"You Marcus?" the bloke who opened the door asked me. "I'm Lamin. The landlord told me meet you and show you room. Is £140 a month and I need 3 months up front, plus another month for deposit."

The smell of the entrance hall reminded me of the damp

under-stairs space at my parents' house. They had a cupboard where a plumber discovered there had a radiator pipe leaking for a number of years. My Dad had reckoned it was due to a natural spring coming out behind the wall, but the truth was a lot less romantic. Lamin's house had a familiar reassuring tang of mold and rotting carpet.

"Don't worry about wet carpet on stairs. He's going to get that fixed", Lamin said ushering me upstairs.

I asked what the deal was with the people who lived in the house.

"Most of them not from London. Some of them don't speak English, so maybe you teach them. I think there 4 or 5 people living here now. Maybe there more sometimes. We don't care so long as they pay rent and don't burn place down."

At the top of the stairs the landing carpet seemed slightly damper under foot. Was that a squelch, or was I imagining it?

"Your room in here" Lamin said, putting a Yale key in a replacement plywood door.

The door opened about half way before it was obstructed by something inside. Lamin beckoned me to squeeze through the gap the door had left me and go in. Good job I wasn't old enough to have gained a middle aged spread. He waited on the landing outside.

Shit. This room was so small that the single bed was put diagonally across it to fit it in. No wonder the door couldn't open, the bed was in the way. Apart from the bed, which had no bedding on it, but quite a few dubious stains, the furniture consisted of one small school chair wedged in the opposite corner. The broken window, which had cracks on each of the four panes, also lacked any form of curtain. I could see through the years of accumulated muck that I had a great view of a brick wall, roughly three feet away.

"The landlord is going to get you some curtains, he said" Lamin nonchalantly added. "So you got money? I need £560." Five hundred and sixty quid? I doubted that Mum and Dad would be able to lend me that much. This was not looking good.

I stepped out of what was earmarked as my box from hell and back onto the landing. A bare bulb flickered above our heads.

Across the landing, through an open door, I could see three other men in their 30s, sitting on a bed. They all looked up at me without any sign of emotion. Each of them had close cropped hair, were dressed in black and I guessed were probably from the Eastern end of the Med. My new neighbours. I had disturbed their card game.

"Don't mind them. They are ones who don't speak English. They won't know what we talking about. We charge them more money because DHS pays them to sit on their arses all day. I hope you not going give me cheque. We like cash. Cash is King."

I was left in a quandary. I had never left home before. I had never rented before. I didn't know if this was normal for London and all part of my adventure. I did know that Richard's accommodation with Mr Biddle was a huge contrast to this shithole. Would I be murdered or mugged if I moved in here? If only I knew someone in London who I could beg to let me occupy a spare room.

I told Lamin that I would go and get his cash. "Four lots of £140 is.....£560? Right? The banks are closed today as it's a Saturday, but my mate has got it and said he would lend it to me until they open. If you wait here, I will go and get the money and be back in an hour."

I never went back. I felt bad about lying to him about my interest, but I didn't want to reject the offer of the room in front of that group of men. Who knows what would have happened to me. Or maybe I just wasn't man enough to say no to his face.

Escaping the house in Kilburn, I realised that my last option was in a road that ran between Kilburn and Willesden Green stations – still in Zone 2 and still just a couple of tube stops away from West Hampstead. I was down to my last 10p, so called the number and suggested that, as the house was literally less than 10 minutes walk, I could come to see the room straight away.

Dartmouth Road is one of those tree lined wide North London suburban through-fares with 1930's houses set back on both sides. It acts as a rat-run that joins Kilburn to Willesden and then up to the North Circular and beyond.

After a ten minute walk, I arrived at number 78 and knocked on the door. No broken glass on this one and the doorstep even looked like it had just been washed, and not with piss this time.

A round, middle-aged women with long ginger hair, wearing a char-woman's pinnie opened the door. I told her I was looking for the owner. She replied that she was indeed the landlady and that I must be the gentleman that just called her. Talk about getting off to a bad start, I had assumed she was the cleaner.

She announced that I was to call her Ann. I had no idea where her accent was from. Was it Eastern European? Maybe Russian or Polish? I couldn't understand one in three words of what she was saying. Her accent wasn't helped by the speed at which she spoke. She was firing out words like a machine gun.

From what I could pick up, I got that I she was offering me my own room in a house full of bedsits. There was no kitchen and I would be sharing a bathroom with five other residents.

My room was on the ground floor next to the front door. Ann opened it up and inside I discovered four magnolia walls, a single bed, and heavy brown wood dressing table, chair and wardrobe. The space felt palatial compared to the box I could have been crammed into just down the road. There was even a two bar electric fire and a small black and white TV which came as part of the rental.

I told Ann that I loved it, and that I was keen to move in quickly as I was starting work the next day. She agreed to take a month's rent, £125, and a month's deposit, meaning that I only had to find £250. I told her I may not be able to get the money to her until Monday after my shift, and she agreed that would be OK.

I walked out of Dartmouth Road for the first time holding a set of keys and a rent book. This weekend trip to London really had taken a bizarre turn.

———

I'd arrived at the house from the Kilburn end of Dartmouth Road, so thought I would kill some time whilst waiting to go back to see Richard after his shift to tell him the good news, by going the other way and checking out the neighbourhood at the far end.

I walked the 7 minutes up towards Willesden Green and carried on past the tube station to find out what my new manor had to offer. The main street was a smaller version of the sprawling mess that was Kilburn High Road, with lots of corner shops, owner-occupier food stores that had their wares spread over the pavement and the standard punctuation marks of bookies and estate agencies.

I thought, OK I'm going to need some stuff and dived into a tatty independent home ware shop, where I picked up two mugs; two half pint glasses; two knives, forks and spoons; a can opener and most importantly of all, a Kenwood kettle. I was now in a position to drink coffee in my room, not least as I had been drinking it black for the last couple of years and didn't need a fridge to store milk.

Armed with my swag, I realised that I still had hours to kill and I needed more change to be able to call home to let my family know the details of the plan to spend my 'year off' working in London.

The obvious solution was to try out the nearest pub. After all if I was to become a local, I may as well get to know all the best places to drink. If I ordered carefully I would end up with a couple of 10ps in my change too. It hadn't occurred to me that I could simply ask someone to change a pound note into coins.

— — — —

The first pub I came to was half way down the High Street. It looked OK from the outside, like many of the pubs back home. The windows had been covered over from the inside, so it was hard to see if it was full of Saturday afternoon drinkers, or if I would be alone in there.

I pushed the door open. My kettle banged on the door frame as I entered, ringing out like a death knell. Fourteen pairs of male eyes watched me walk across the sawdust covered concrete floor, as I went across what seemed like a gaping void to get to the bar. No one was talking. Each man was too busy staring at the person who had just walked in, who they had indeed never seen before. A lad in Kickers, with red cheeks and a terrible haircut, carrying a kettle. Irish eyes weren't smiling.

The bar was draped with the green, orange and white of Ireland and images of leprechauns and shamrocks adorned the mirrors behind the optic shelf. A tune came out of a speaker covered in cobwebs, which I later learned was called 'Maids when you're young, never wed an old man' by the Dubliners. Good advice.

"What'll you be having?" the overweight barman in an emerald green football shirt asked me, cleaning a pint glass with a cloth, a cigarette hanging from the corner of his mouth.

I asked for a pint of lager. "Lager. That'll be that drink we serve to the ladies when they come in", he replied without a hint of humour. He was being deadly serious.

We exchanged cash for a ladies' drink and I took a seat near to the door. The fourteen men in the bar continued to silently stare at me whilst I took a first tentative sip. It was obvious that they didn't serve many ladies as the lager tasted more of cleaning fluid than hops, or barley. I wondered if they could tell that my wrist was trembling as I picked up the glass. I wondered if the fact that I needed to use both hands to lift it confirmed what they already knew, that I was scared shitless of the situation I had naively wondered into.

When I was at school, the only wasted alcohol was the odd glass of beer or wine that got spilled at parties. We all subscribed to the theory that not a drop would go down the plughole. This stuff was hard to come by after all for two reasons. Firstly the cost and secondly, the fact that all of us were underage drinkers and had to come up with schemes that would gain access to booze (or discover which pubs would turn a blind eye if Danny's dad wasn't involved).

Sitting here in the pub I had a decision to make. Continue to drink and keep an eye on the unwelcoming party, or subtly put my drink back on the beer mat and make my excuses and leave. I decided to get the hell out of there whilst I was in one piece.

So the three quarter full pint glass went back on the table, I picked up my bag of shopping and stood up to make my exit. I was half way through the door when I heard, "Hey poofter, come back in here and you can suck my dick!" in the broad Irish accent I had listened to many times on TV documentaries about the troubles in Ireland. I declined the offer and beat a hasty retreat back to my new home, stopping only briefly to buy a jar of Maxwell House and a couple of Twix bars. That'll be dinner sorted.

I had survived my first 24 hours in London. I had got a job and somewhere to sleep. It was actually good news that rent and travel would eat up most of my pay and that I would be unlikely to be able to return to a pub to buy expensive drinks again. After my brush with the IRA, or was it the UDF, I was glad that all I was going to have to look forward to would be a can of Castlemaine bought in the offie on high days and holidays.

So I made my first cup of coffee, which tasted disgusting. Was it the coffee, I had never drank anything other than Nescafe before, or maybe the water from the bathroom tap? Maybe the kettle needed time to get used to doing its job? Perhaps it was the new black mug. My second coffee was it the white mug with red stripes and it tasted better. To this day, 40 years on, I never drink coffee from black cups or mugs. If someone makes me one at their house, I have to ask to pour it into another of any other colour. In fact I would rather go without a caffeine fix than have it from a black mug. I must associate them with nearly being beaten to death by the drinkers in Willesden Green.

Which is irrational, on so many levels.

———

I decided to walk over to Richard's, after all he lived at the next stop on the tube and that could only be a half mile away.

Having never really used an A to Z before, other than looking up locations of potential bedsits, I went a bit of a long way round, via Finchley Road and Swiss Cottage, before I realised I was lost and asked in a shop for directions. What should have been a 15 minute walk at most, ended up being an hour and a half, most of which was spent thinking, if I ever get back to Dartmouth Road, I will probably head straight to Paddington afterwards.

The sun had set by the time I got to his digs and he was back from work. He welcomed me in and I gave him a prolonged version of the events of that day. I tried to sound interesting in return, but he didn't try to hide his boredom. Each part of my saga was punctuated with "Fucking Buddle has run out of tea bags. That bastard Buddle hasn't got any pasta. Do you want one of his pizzas? Here, have a beer, Buddle doesn't count them. He'll be back from his book club soon, so if you want to take anything like toothpaste from his bathroom drawers, now would be a good time to do it" and other comments about how he was being wronged by his brother's friend who was only trying to do right by him.

"How much money do you have?" Richard asked. I told him after the expense of traveling around North West London and buying the essentials I had the grand total of £3.47 to last me until I could get to a bank on Monday. Out of that I would need to buy a tube ticket into work in the morning and keep some back for food tomorrow too, bearing in mind that all the shops would be shut on Sunday. Also I had to make a call to my parents to tell them I wouldn't be coming home. In other words, I was nearly skint.

"Ah, not enough for two beers down the pub then. Tell you what. If you go into Buddle's study he's got a phone in there. You can call your parents and save yourself a large slice of dosh."

I went back into the musty, chaotic, book filled room and found an old Bakelite dial phone underneath a copy of Private Eye lying on his desk. For a moment I wondered if that was some kind of trap to alert Mr Biddle to the fact that Richard and been abusing his phone bill.

Calling Mum and Dad would be a bit tricky. I'd need to get the right tone, upbeat enthusiasm without this sounding a bit manic and crazy. I had not been abducted by aliens, nor white slave traders, but for some equally mad reason had let Richard talk me into working in London for the next few months, to mark time whilst waiting to hear back from my Uni and Poly applications. I'd try to get home in a couple of weeks to pick up some more clothes and other useful items. Like an iron and my ghetto blaster. Or more pants even.

Obviously, this was the first time I had been away from home and I started to think about a few practicalities whilst talking to Mum. How do I get my clothes washed and how often? Clothes at home seemed to disappear from my bedroom floor and reappear clean in the wardrobe. I'd probably have to go to a launderette, like the ones I used to go to with Mum when I was about ten, before they could afford a machine on my Dad's apprenticeship wages. I remember how we would buy a cup of powder and sit and watch the clothes tumble and fall.

Mum was quite surprised and encouraging in equal measure. Her main concern was whether or not I would have enough money until I got paid, which I hadn't actually thought about. Well not to the level of detail Mum wanted me to anyway. She suggested that she sent me a cheque first thing on Monday morning, made out to my landlady, to cover my rent. I was hoping that she would come to this conclusion, as I was too proud to ask her for cash.

As I hadn't thought to ask Ann's surname, we agreed on a signed blank cheque and I could fill in the details later. She said she would also put an extra cheque in the post that I could use as a loan until I got paid.

She then wanted to know how close I was to Peckham. I told her I had no idea. She told me how a friend of hers' son, who I vaguely knew, had been mugged four times in the last two weeks. Two of those times were on the tube going back to his accommodation.

That was reassuring. The only good news about that story was that the lad, John, had always had the reputation of being a total wimp when we knew him as kids. The stories I'd heard about him since only confirmed that. This was the boy who used to keep his Matchbox cars in their boxes and never really played with any of his toys – he liked to keep them untouched in mint condition. He also had a massive collection of war comics that I used to read instead of playing with him. I'm sure he's since made a fortune on eBay, or has a room that houses his collections, that no one is allowed to go in unless they wear white gloves.

I told Mum that I was way more street wise than John (I wasn't) and that being more than 6 feet tall (the same height as him) it was unlikely anyone would try anything. I would keep an eye out for trouble and go around London looking confident even if I didn't feel it. Muggers always single out people who didn't look like they knew where they were going and John probably had 'victim' written all over him. I'd make sure I didn't look at my A to Z when anyone was watching and develop an expression that said, 'Don't fuck with me, please'.

Finishing the call, I felt like the umbilical cord hadn't been cut, but the 110 miles between us has given it a good stretch.

I went back downstairs to find Mr Biddle stood in the kitchen doorway. He was dressed in a dusty black needle cord suit and his scraggy sandy hair didn't quite hide his paisley patterned neckerchief. He wasn't aware I was behind him. I could see Richard in the kitchen sat holding half a slice of cheese and tomato pizza in mid air.

"I would appreciate it if you replaced the food you eat Richard. I agreed with your brother to rent you my spare room, but I didn't agree to you having free access to the contents of my kitchen cupboard as well. Also, when is your friend moving off my sofa? Correct me if I'm wrong, but did I agree to him staying here?"

I coughed slightly. Just enough for him to realise that he had an audience. Don't worry Mr Biddle, I've already moved out. I'm just here collecting my stuff.

"Come on Marcus. Let's take a walk", Richard suggested.

We left the house and started to stroll along the wet pavements, which must have been exposed to a shower whilst I had been thinking about stealing soap from Mr Biddle's bathroom.

"Get used to this mate. People will try to screw you over in this town. And, there is nothing to do here without money. Apart from playing guitar and walking. I have no money, so I do a lot of walking. I said walking, with an l not an n! These

47

are my best entertainment." Richard slapped his thighs as if he was playing the lead in a pantomime.

We turned right onto West Hampstead's High Street and started strolling up the hill. I realised that Richard moved a lot quicker than I would do naturally and rather than him relaxing his pace, I was having to try to keep up. I was slightly out of breath. Despite my obvious lack of fitness, Richard showed no sign of slowing down for me.

The shop fronts were in total contrast to those I had seen earlier in the day, less than a mile away in Kilburn. Stores were closed for the night, but their windows still oozed wealth and the people meandering past us all looked equally moneyed. On their way to a posh meal or to get richly sizzled in a cocktail bar no doubt, before having very expensive and yet equally unfulfilling sex in their £1M flats. We were both hopeful about the unfulfilled part, otherwise we would have been properly jealous.

"Well I stand up next to a mountain. And I chop it down with the edge of my hand", Richard muttered under his breath. We were a couple of voodoo children, who didn't mean to take up anyone's sweet time. Our ordinariness made us disappear from the gaze of the local residents. How do people get to be so rich? We discussed that for half an hour before I told him I was heading 'home' and Richard pointed me in the right direction. This time I was pretty sure I could get back without getting lost, or mugged.

Before I knew it, I was under the cold nylon sheets and blankets in my room. There was an eerie orange glow across the ceiling, coming from the street light outside. It all felt like a massive mistake.

Day 1

Nervous? Me? You bet. Day one of my job and not a clue what to expect.

Just after waking, there was a knock on the door. Ann stood there holding a tray.

"I don't know if you have a kettle yet, but here's a coffee for you for your first day."

It was a kind gesture, even if the coffee was milky and undrinkable. Ann had also added a cheese sandwich to the tray, which seemed like an odd choice for breakfast. White sliced bread and cheddar. Maybe that was standard breakfast where she came from. As I said, it was a kind gesture.

Richard had talked me through how to 'legally' fare dodge the tubes. As I lived between two stops, I could go to one of them in the morning and buy a ticket to the other one. That would get me onto the platform and get me off at the other station when I came home later in the day.

Then I just needed a Zone 1 weekly pass - which had a hefty discount applied – that would allow me to get on and off the tube at Bond Street and I could use it to go places on my day off too. The only risk would be if an inspector got on in between Kilburn and the Central Zone – which was only two stops - and if that happened, I was to say I had fallen asleep and missed my station.

There was a time/date stamp printed on the ticket I bought at Willesden Green in the morning. But it was so small that the guy on the ticket booth at Kilburn wouldn't notice it, as I would be one of a crowd of commuters handing him tickets as we walked through past his box. And if for some reason he wasn't there in the evening, I'd keep the ticket and use it the following morning – an extra bonus saving, if not upping the risk of punishment if I was caught.

Thanks to tube stations not having any barriers, unlike the automatic gates they have nowadays, this money saving exercise was pretty simple to achieve. Imagine being able to walk on and off tube stations unchallenged. The Underground must have lost millions thanks to fare dodgers. I'd joined the petty criminal fraternity.

What I was doing wasn't really illegal, like so many other people who simply walked on and off stations. At least I had a ticket to hand in and was making a contribution to my travel, even if was slightly less of one than David Howell, the Minister for Transport, would want from me.

I'd do this just as soon as Mum's money showed up. It was Day One and I only had enough to pay for a full fare return ticket into London. So my life of crime would have to be postponed, at least until I could afford a weekly Central Zone pass. It did seem a bit bizarre that I would only be able to save money, once I had more money. But that was the nature of the fiddle.

I got off the tube at Bond Street. Went up the escalator and into the ticket concourse, which seemed to be the basement of a small shopping centre. None of the shops were open, it was Sunday after all.

I turned right and then right again out of the back door of

the W1 Centre and found myself in Duke Street. Must be the same Duke Street that had a Duchess. I vaguely remembered some TV drama about an Victorian cook of the same name.

There was the hotel again. A tall building with hundreds of white-framed windows. The guy who had let me in before my interview was stood next to a black Rolls Royce with small flags on the bonnet, parked in the drop-off bay in front of the heavy doors that he was in charge of.

"Side entrance. Guests only through here."

I found the staff entrance and squeezed though the small doorway into a concrete floored, off-white tiled corridor that led to an equally austere flight of concrete stairs. Inside a glass box an old man welcomed me through a window in the protective screen.

"You new? Clock in and I'll tell the staff department you are here."

Clock in? What the hell did that mean? I stood there for a couple of minutes and another, more established staff member came in. She took a card from the wall behind her, which was covered in alphabetised slots, and fed hers into the mouth of a metal box with a clock face on it. It made a thumping noise and she took the card out and placed it in a similar metal frame on the opposite wall.

I looked on wall number one and there was my card. It was easy to spot as it was clean compared to the others, even if my name was spelled incorrectly on the top. I still hate people that use a K instead of a C. Komplete kunts.

I fed the machine. It clunked and a red time stamp appeared, printed at the top of my card. I was now officially a worker.

Shortly afterwards the man who had conducted my interview two days before appeared. He greeted me with, "I thought I told you to get a haircut?" I reassured him that was in hand and would be sorted later that night. I had never been to a barber in my life, my Mum had always cut my hair, and I was too scared to go to one – what would I ask for if I did? Weren't barber shops all full of singing quartets, or sleazy old men who wanted to know if they could sell you condoms for the weekend?

So it would have to be another first - a self-inflicted hair cut. I realised that my promise would only be met if I could find a pair of scissors later that day.

I followed my host down the bare flight of stone stairs into what I assumed was the underbelly of the hotel. There seemed to be a lot of shouting and things being bashed about, although I couldn't see where the noise was coming from. We continued to walk along an over-lit corridor with bare fluorescent tubes at eye level. A lot of cables had been strung up in the ceiling. I was sure that some of them were sparking above me. It felt like I was entering some East German cold war bunker and I was surprised that the people pushing trolleys full of dirty plates and cages piled high with used towels were not wearing Russian army uniforms.

I realised that I was being taken into the Staff Department through a back entrance and was soon in the same small room I had been interviewed in less than two days before.

"Now. Here's your paperwork. You need to sign this contract. Sorry we're starting you on a Sunday, it means that you'll miss the first day training session that we run. You won't need it anyway. All we talk about is dress code and security and show you a video."

"Dress code needs some work. We've talked about your hair being on your shoulders and you probably should think about investing in an iron. I imagine you're too young to shave every day, but the fluff needs to go too. You won't be seeing any guests today, and not for a while until your department is set up, so don't worry about looking like a scruffy bastard. Yet. I'm not going to give you a formal warning today." I wasn't sure if his smirk was a prompt for me to laugh, or if he was amusing himself by being cruel.

So I kept schtum. Any remaining self-belief would be walking out of the door without me.

"Security. The simple rule is that if you nick anything from the hotel, we will chop your bollocks off. You know that you have to clock in and out of the staff entrance. If you get anyone to do that for you, because you are still in bed with a hangover, you can expect the same treatment. Cheating the clock will result in instant dismissal."

I admitted I hadn't even considered either option, but re-alised it must be an ongoing problem, given the importance he was placing on it. I wasn't really sure what 'instant dismissal' meant, but it sounded pretty terminal. I also wondered how many bollocks he had in a jar somewhere in the filing.

"I'm supposed to talk to you about health and safety. Easy one that. Just don't have an accident and if you do, then put it in the book." He held up a tatty exercise book with a yellow paper cover.

"Another thing. We put staff members from other hotels in rooms every now and then, to try to bribe our people. So if anyone offers you a massive tip, it's probably one of our people. Do not take it. If anyone suggests that you stop doing what you are doing and go to their room to do them instead, then it's probably one of our people. Do not do it. You won't get your end away, you'll just get fired. If you say yes to either of these situations, you know where your bollocks will end up and it won't be down the throat of one of our members of staff."

I caught myself starting to blush. I was a country boy, who had obviously led a very sheltered life. Nothing like this had ever happened to me. I think the closest I had got to such excitement before was spending an evening at a sixth form house party, in the spare bedroom underneath a pile of coats with Tricia, who had the reputation of liking all the boys.

"Oh yes. The rest of your uniform. Here's a black bow tie. It just clips onto your collar. You have to wear that at all times, even when you are not in guest areas. Before you ask, the reason why it clips on is to save you being strangled by any angry guest or another member of staff. We had a situation once with a bow tie that went around the waiter's neck and nearly ended up being his noose. It wasn't pleasant and ended up with a spilled tray of flaming Sambucas that caused an expensive repair to the dining room carpet." I wondered what a flaming Sambuca was. Whatever they were, having a proper tie on sounded dangerous.

"Here's your jacket. I took a guess at extra large. Try it on. Looks like you've not got much muscle on you and it's too big. But either you'll grow into it, or you can swap it with someone else in Floor Service. Or you can just wait until someone decides what uniform the Mini-Bar crew should wear and we can order you a proper costume. Your team is known as the scruffiest bunch of wankers in the hotel, so you'll fit right in."

I was starting to think that Staff Department members didn't like being asked to come in on a Sunday to induct new people.

"Any questions?"

I asked how I could book some time off in a couple of weeks, so I could go back to Gloucestershire to collect my belongings. I didn't mention my seeing my family, as I knew it would make me seem soft and would do little else other than to confirm his view of me as a scruffy wanker.

"You get paid holiday from year two. So you have to work a year first. We do give you Bank Holidays, but obviously we are open on all of those. So they fall into the rota like any other day. We give you a day off in lieu. Your department boss can give you up to 20 days a year unpaid in your first year, but that's discretionary. If he needs you to work, then tough. If I were you mate I would be worrying about showing some commitment to the cause, rather than planning your next sex on the beach."

Must be code for something. I'd never had sex on a beach before, not even with Alison when we stayed in Northern Spain for a couple of weeks at her aunt's.

Oh. Ah well. Maybe I could persuade Mum or Dad to do a drive up to London for me, or I would have to find a department store that sold underpants.

Alison would be a bit more difficult. She had gone to Leeds University a few weeks before and, by the sound of her letters, was having an amazing time. I needed time to get up to Leeds to show Ali that I was still her man and for her to come down to London so I could take her to Garfunkels, and maybe even save up some cash to get some theatre tickets. I was in the West End after all and I needed to show her I was worth the hassle. It seemed that getting enough time off to service our threadbare relationship would be virtually impossible.

Before I went I had another question. What were we doing in on a Sunday, if Monday was the usual start day? I thought that was being a bit clever and may put my adversary on his back foot.

"Simple. Your team were given a deadline of last week to get the mini-bars installed in all the rooms of this hotel. They are still two floors short. They've blamed it on the service trolleys being stuck in Switzerland, but I think they've just been working too slow. So the Hotel Manager has canceled any days off for your team until each room has a fully-functioning fridge, full of executive booze. Good luck with that one!"

I asked why the trolleys were in Switzerland when we were obviously in London.

"It's where they manufacture them, numpty. They are just massive metal boxes on wheels. Apparently no one in Britain has the skill to make them. Which is a bit sad really."

So, having been intimidated, abused and emasculated for 15 minutes, I was now officially inducted.

———

A phone call and five minutes more of embarrassed silence, before a knock on the door and in walked Ahmet Ekmekci.

Ahmet introduced himself to me as the Assistant Mini-Bar Manager. As I stood up I realised that he could only be about 5 feet 2. "You're a big lad, the boys are going to love you", Ahmet remarked.

I put on my jacket and after a bit of fiddling, clicked the bow tie into place. Ready to go, I collected the paperwork from the desk in front of me, which had now been put into a cardboard folder with a picture of the hotel on the front. The words 'Jupiter Hotel Induction Pack' were typed on to a piece of paper stuck on the top corner.

Ahmet beckoned me to follow him and a couple of steps later we were in the staff lift, or the 'service lift' as he called it. I wondered why the lift was just outside the door of the Staff Department – probably so they could keep an eye on who was going up and down. Either that or it was to give them quick access if they needed to get upstairs to castrate someone.

"What's your name again?" I confirmed I was still called Markus.

"I'm Ahmet. I live in Romford, I'm a DJ and I've been working here for a couple of years. I got moved from Floor Service to the Mini-Bars when it got set up in the summer. Seemed like a good idea at the time. There are only so many a-holes you can take so much abuse from." I wondered if he meant the guests or the people he used to work with.

"The Mini-Bar department office is on the top floor. Which is class because the hotel gets filled up from the bottom. We will only have guests up there with us when we're really busy. Just before Christmas and a few weekends. Rest of the time it's our floor, apart from the Housekeepers who also have an office up there at the other end of our corridor. You'll get to meet them. Are you gay?"

Well hello to you too, Ahmet. I said I had a girlfriend at Leeds University.

Ahmet whistled through his teeth and looked down his long hooked nose at me. Which was quite an achievement given he was about a foot shorter.

"Intelligent one eh? I hope you're not planning to go to university. We fucking hate students working here."

I reassured him that I had wanted to, but I had spent too much time in the pub to get the grades. This seemed to impress him and I saw his very broad smile for the first time. A mouth full of white teeth.

"You're going to fit in well with us. We're a load of fucking wasters. I don't think that any of us have even got any O Levels. But what we lack in school brains, we make up for

in street brains. You need street brains if you live in Romford."
I couldn't comment on that. I didn't want to insult him by
asking if Romford was anywhere near Brixton, where the riots
had happened a couple of years before.

The service lift doors clunked open and we turned sharply
into a dimly lit hallway. Deep red carpet, brown and orange
wallpaper and heavy, dark brown guest room doors, each
numbered and starting with 6. Lighting units were set into
the walls in between each room. The decor looked like some of
the faded memories of the 1970s captured in my parents' photo
album, before the advent of punk and the concept of interior
design.

I asked Ahmet if this was the 6th floor.

"Clever lad. You sure you're not going to university?" he
replied with a broad grin.

At the end of the corridor was an open door with white
light coming from it, as well as the sound of a tinny radio.
Outside the room were two very large gunmetal gray metal
boxes on wheels that had shutters pulled down on the sides.
They partially blocked the corridor space and I could see that it
would be difficult for guests to squeeze past. I guessed correctly
that they had something to do with the Mini-Bar team - they
had the look of something Swiss - functional and serious and
there was a reason they had been parked on a floor where the
guests very rarely stepped foot.

Ahmet led me into the Mini-Bar office.

"Welcome home. Guys, this is Marcus. Marcus - these are
the gays." Was that the Romford accent or a Freudian slip?

A man and three youths sat in front of me. The three younger
faces occupied the only three chairs in the space and the older
guy perched on the table.

He offered me his right hand. I noticed the silver cuff link with an embedded jewel on his shirt sleeve as I shook it. He was tall, gaunt, probably somewhere in his late 30s, or early 40s. His piercing blue eyes looked like they had a great deal of sadness in them. His slightly receding black hair was way longer at the back than I had been advised was acceptable and his sallow smoker's skin made him look like a character from The Godfather. Probably more of a minor gangster than full family.

He took a drag on his cigarette.

"Hello. What's your name?"

I told him.

"Marco. I'm going to call you Marco. It's short for Marcus isn't it?" I told him I didn't think so, but if that's what he wanted to call me that was fine, I had been called a lot worse in my time, even just in my time in London and mainly in the Staff Department of the hotel.

The three stooges on the chairs smirked.

"I'm Joe Makris. Before you ask, I'm from Malta. I used to be in Floor Service, and now I am your Manager here. Someone must have thought I was an asshole in Floor Service, so they gave me Ahmet and told me to put fridges in all the rooms. If you behave yourself, one day you could end up like me. If you want to have a fucking sad life working with this bunch of wankers, work hard and you can be the boss when I retire in 25 time."

"These three guys are Andrew, John-Mick and Didier. John-Mick and Didier are French. Andrew is just a massive English poof. He doesn't mind us calling him that." (He obviously did).

"As I said John-Mick and Didier are French, so they are probably massive poofs as well. I haven't found out if that's

59

true yet, have I boys?" Didier smirked again and John-Mick did a Gallic shrug of the shoulders.

"Let me explain what we do here." Joe continued in his heavy Eastern Med accent. "Mr Philiposis is the bastard who now runs Floor Service. One time he visited a friend at another hotel in London and that bastard showed him a fridge in a room. 'Get these fridges' they said, 'think of all the times you take booze to your guests. They can help themselves. Your boys can sit in the Floor Service office and play with their dicks instead'. Mr P thought, 'Yeah that's a great idea. I will find a couple of suckers who can set up my fridges'."

"So he had a fridge put in all 280 rooms in the hotel and asked me and Ahmet to fill those little fuckers. We've been filling them for weeks. Every time we get a floor filled, people start drinking what's inside, so we have to refill them. All the time, Mr P is saying 'Why are my Floor Service guys still getting asked for whiskey at 2 am? I'll tell you why Joe, because your fuckers haven't filled up the mini-bars like I told you to'."

"The Big Manager never leaves the ground floor, but he came up to see me and told me to get them filled or else my bollocks would be dangling from the office window. I reckon Mr P had been in the ear of the Big Manager, as well as up his arse. We are six floors up, so I'm going to get them filled. I don't mind telling Mr P to fuck off, but the Big Guy...no. He's the man in charge."

"And you are going to help me." Joe placed his hand on my shoulder and looked at me as if he was about to whisper a secret. "You, Marco, are now one of my boys. If you are a good boy I will be your good Daddy. But if you dick me about, don't expect me to be nice."

"Break over. Back to work. Andrew, take Marco with you to

60

refill floors one and two. Show him all the paperwork. The rest of you can get on to floor four and start filling fridges. Have we got enough clean glasses? I'll join you, but I need to go and talk to housekeeping first. Oh yeah, Marco, you'll need this. They live in this room at night and we lock them in here, so don't get any funny ideas."

He threw a piece of white plastic to me. It was about 6 inches long and 2 wide. One end had a series of holes punched in it. I had no idea what it was, but realised it must be important, as there were two small keys attached to it. I clipped it onto my belt.

Andrew gestured to me to go outside into the corridor. He was a diminutive chap with black hair cut into a Freddie Mercury style to match his moustache. His dark brown eyes mirrored his equally dark and bushy eyebrows. I thought he must be just a couple of years older than me at most. Obviously a fan of Queen too.

Interestingly, instead of our Floor Service burgundy jackets, he wore a white one that buttoned right across his front, similar to those I had seen chefs wear at the Harvester back home when they were slicing the three types of meat.

"Eh. Hello, I'm Andrew." I couldn't place his accent, but thought he sounded like a couple of people I knew back home who had moved from Manchester, although with Andrew all his vowels seemed a bit sharpened and his sentences were prone to rising at the end. A bit nasal too.

"You're probably wondering why I don't have a Floor Service jacket like the rest of you." I was.

"Eh. I used to work in the Grill Bar downstairs as a commis-waiter. But I wanted a promotion. When the Mini-Bars opened I jumped at the chance." I thought it better not to ask why he had been a communist waiter, so I questioned what his relationship to Joe and Ahmet was instead. It felt like this team had a lot of chiefs and I wasn't sure if Andrew was one of them.

"No. Eh. I'm the same as you, a Mini-Bar Attendant. I see it as a step up as I was a commis-waiter before."

There is was again. I wondered how filling fridges was any more important than delivering diners' orders and how a 'commie' waiter was any different from a waiter. He must be missing his old job, as he seemed to have mentionitis. Maybe Andrew was still a communist.

"So before we go on to the floor, we have to fill up our trolley." The big metal box on wheels outside the office. "These things only came from Switzerland the day before yesterday. We were using the Floor Service trolleys, which are very, very small. It made our jobs very, very difficult. I like these big ones." He continued.

"Each trolley has the same amount of stock on it. Eh. That way we know when we're finished how much we've used and that should match up to our billing dockets too." He showed me a pad of triplicate forms, each listing stock items with a space to enter number used and the room number at the top.

"When we get back to the office, we key all our dockets into the terminal and the accounts people add them to the guests' bills. Eh. Most problems come when guests check out before we have had a chance to check their mini-bars or process their dockets. Reception goes mental when that happens."

"I had a day of work experience on the Front Desk when I was hoping to get a move out of the restaurant a couple of years ago. Eh. The Receptionists hate Floor Service for the same reason, although Floor Service dockets only fail to get processed if the waiters are being too lazy. For us it's worse because we don't even know our guests have been in the fridge. So Reception thinks we are scum."

I hadn't quite understood most of what he was saying. It seemed that we basically wrote out a bill each time we filled up a fridge in a room and the key to the whole thing was to get those charged to the rooms through the accounts system before the guest checked out. No degree needed for that one.

I was also beginning to realise that there was a pecking order in this place and wondered if Mini-Bars were at the bottom. It turned out we were well below the elite Receptionists and Concierge, a good few miles below the Housekeepers, slightly below the Chambermaids and Floor Service waiters and just a few paces behind the hospitality waiting staff. But hey good news! The kitchen staff were below us (quite literally as they occupied most of the basement – hence the noise I heard when I first arrived) and the Porters were right at the bottom of pile. People didn't even swear at them when they saw them, as they would do to the Mini-Bars. They were THAT low in the pecking order that they weren't even acknowledged.

Andrew used one of the small keys to unlock the shutters of the trolley. "You have to keep the doors down and locked every time you leave it", he explained. "We were using Floor Service trolleys until yesterday which are tables on wheels. I'm sure that a few of our miniatures were nicked by the Floor Service waiters when we were in the rooms filling fridges. My advice to you - don't trust those guys. They are a bunch of thieves."

He made a list of the items missing from his trolley and took me back into the small office. Shelving along one wall contained our stock items. Rows of small bottles of spirits, a couple of crates of micro orange juices, and 25ml cans of Coke and 7Up. There were also some brown card boxes with bags of peanuts inside them.

"Now then. Eh. I need: 3 Smirnoff; 4 Jim Beam; 2 Chivas; 4 Cokes..." and the list went on. I realised that Andrew was in fact talking to himself rather than to me. He loaded his order into the slots of the trolley and slammed down the shuttered door. He made a point of locking it and reminding me of the importance of doing so, just in case I had forgotten what he had said less than five minutes ago.

"Eh. Did anyone tell you that we didn't do anything for three weeks when we first set up the Mini-Bar team because half of the stock hadn't been ordered? All there was to do was cleaning glasses and mopping the office floor. That was before the French guys started. So it was just me washing glasses and me mopping the floor for three weeks, whilst Ahmet and Joe were getting drunk with the Housekeepers. People in the rest of the hotel think we're lazy. It's not our fault that we had fridges, but nothing to put in them."

I found out later that it was indeed our fault. Joe and Ahmet had both assumed that the stock had been ordered by the other one, and they were too drunk to realise their mistake until almost a couple of weeks in when Mr P broke up the party.

He pushed the trolley away from the office and towards the service lift. It was obviously very heavy. I asked him if he needed a hand, but he just gave me a look which translated as 'are you kidding me' or worse. I had been glared at by a mini-Freddie Mercury for doubting his strength, and it felt slightly odd.

————

The lift descended to the first floor. The double doors opened and I realised that the combined weight of the two of us and the trolley must have stretched the lift's cable, as there was now a step out of it of about two inches. I asked Andrew if that was anything to be worried about. Given that we were only a floor up I calculated that we'd probably survive if the cable snapped, but at least one of us would get crushed by the trolley.

"No. It just means that it's easy to push this beast into the lift, eh, but you have to work hard to pull it out." We manoeuvred around it and gave it a tug over the threshold. As Andrew had said, the trolley was fairly simple to extract with two of us pulling. It popped out with a meaningful rattle of the bottles that were contained within it.

"We are the champions my friend. And we'll keep on pulling to the end!", I declared as the lift doors closed behind us. Andrew gave me a look that made it clear that the Queen reference had missed the mark. His mercurial image must have been a coincidence.

The first floor looked exactly the same as the sixth, although it was more alive. Open room doors gave glimpses of chamber-maids making the beds; trays were left on the corridor carpet for collection by the Floor Service staff later – but not until Mr P arrived for work and sent his troops out on their morning foraging mission; various newspapers still sat outside rooms that had DO NOT DISTURB signs hanging on their door handles.

Andrew guided the trolley to one end of the corridor, next to room 101.

"101 and 102 are a suite. I happen to know that the people who stay there when they are in London are not in this country at the moment, so this is an easy one. Eh. Just go in there and see if the fridge seal is still intact."

I wondered what that meant, so Andrew held up a strip of

paper. One side was printed with the hotel logo on a brown background along with the words, "Your Mini-Bar has been serviced." On the back was a gummed area. The idea was that these were to be stuck over the seal of the fridge door and it would serve as an easy way to spot if it had been used.

Of course, like most things in that hotel, the glue on the back of the seal was inadequate and most of the strips would fall off, even when there had been no guest in the room. Despite the team raising this with Joe, he didn't have the inclination to raise it higher up to get an alternative sorted out. Some of the guests would take the contents and stick the strips back onto the fridge to reseal it, only for the next guest to pick up the bill. It was a rubbish system. So eventually the strips would end up in one of the empty peanut boxes as a souvenir of times gone by and every fridge would need a manual check, every day.

Andrew pointed at the door of 101. It felt appropriate that my first fridge check was for this room number and I made the observation to him. He looked at me quizzically and said, "I don't get it. Eh. Do you mean because it is the first room in the hotel, or something else?" When I explained the Orwellian reference, he replied, "Are you planning to go to university? They hate people who go to university in this hotel. Do you know that I haven't even opened a book since I was 15? That was 'Rainbow, the Stormy Life of Judy Garland'. Have you read it? You should. It is excellent. All about Judy Garland".

I told him I hadn't (and wondered if he was taking the piss). I was reading an Italo Calvino and recommended it to him. The suggestion seemed to pass straight through him. I wondered if he read magazines or newspapers. Again a no. Perhaps we should just stick to the job in hand.

I then realised what the piece of plastic on the end on an

elastic lanyard was for. Joe was right, I did need it. It was the master key and would get me into any guest room in the hotel. I went to slot the key into the lock, but Andrew grabbed my arm.

"No. First you have to knock and call 'Mini-Bars'. If there is no reply you can open the door. Unless of course there is a Do Not Disturb sign, in which case you have to come back later. Eh. My rule of thumb if there is tray outside, they're out of bed, so I knock regardless."

So I knocked and shouted 'Mini-Bars'. It seemed a bit mad as Andrew had already told me that the room was empty. But he was one for the rules and I should really follow them on my first day at work.

The room was huge. This was the premium space of the premium hotel after all. I could see Grosvenor Square and the US Embassy through the net curtains. Andrew walked over to a brown fake wood laminated box a couple of feet tall and a foot or so wide, which was sat under the dressing table.

"This is a mini-bar", he proudly announced as if he was revealing a national secret to me. He then took the other key from his lanyard and opened it.

"Now I know for a fact that this mini-bar is complete. Partly because it was sealed, see." He held up the strip of brown paper which was now broken in two. "I also knew that the guests weren't here. But I won't tell you how I know that. Eh. Only to say that I still have friends on Reception and I have a particular interest in the regular guest who stays here", he said cryptically.

Maybe Andrew's one day failed trial on the front desk had been useful to him after all. Either that or he was playing mind games with me. I doubted that he had a hot-line to the usual occupant, unless he led a secret double life. Stranger things have happened.

Having cleared out of the palatial rooms 101/102, our next visit was 103. I won't bore you with a list of which rooms had what, as Andrew would, but suffice to say that by the time we had got to the end of the first floor nearly three hours later, I had got into the swing of opening doors, not opening doors, checking the fridges, getting refills from the trolley and writing out the dockets.

I noticed that Andrew waddled rather than walked. With his white jacket and black trousers and shoes, he really did look like a penguin. I wondered whether John-Mick and Didier's English was good enough to get the joke if I made it. Probably not on day 1. Keep your Frenchmen close, and your penguins closer.

Andrew suggested we had a break for lunch before moving on to Floor 2 for our afternoon of checking. He seemed to suggest that the longer we took over that floor the better, as it would mean less time with the rest of the squad at the end of the day filling the new bars. He complained that Ahmet kept telling him that he filled them too slowly. He just wanted to take his time and make sure everything 'looked nice'.

We locked the trolley at the end of the second floor and jumped back into the service lift to the basement.

I could smell the kitchens and what turned out to be lunch before I got there. It seemed that the hotel recognised that it paid its staff such small amounts that it was willing to feed them. Had it not, then I imagine a lot of hotel workers would be keeling over with malnutrition.

The staff cafe was Spartan, with banks of long plastic tables and chairs more akin to a underground army mess hall. The deal was grab a tray, get your food from a hatch and then sit with your mates. I could see that for Andrew that was going to be a problem, so he suggested the two of us sat at one end of an empty table for eight.

"Do you like teeth?" he asked me as we sat down to face our shepherds pies. I think my expression gave him my answer: 'What?!'

"I hate teeth. I hate my teeth. If I didn't have teeth I would be really happy. Before I moved down to London I asked my dentist if he could pull all of my teeth out, but he wouldn't do it unless there was a medical reason. Eh. I told him my medical reason was that I don't like having them. But he said that was a *mental* reason and I should go and see someone else about that. Probably a shrink. 'Can they pull out teeth?', I said. 'No. But they can sort out your head', he replied. But people tell me that my head is good, and that's one of the reasons I wanted my teeth out in the first place!"

I didn't understand the last comment - surely only mentalists want all their teeth pulled out. I enquired what the problem was.

"Wouldn't you prefer to have an empty mouth? You wouldn't need to worry about cleaning them and you'd be able to get a lot more in if they weren't in the way. Of course you would need false ones for when you wanted to eat something."

I was starting to realise why Andrew was a bit of a Billy-No-Mates. This conversation was more bizarre than any I could remember having back home. We used to joke about what it would be like to have fingers for a penis etc, but that was pub talk and entirely hypothetical. I was talking to a man who was contemplating what he thought to be serious self-improvement surgery.

What did he mean about being able to get more in? More of what? Would he walk around with his false teeth in his pocket ready for his lunch break? What about the rest of the time?

Halfway through the lunch-break another man in a burgundy jacket walked past our table. "Karl, Karl! Come and sit with us Karl", Andrew called out to him. Karl must have been deaf as he carried on walking to the other end of the room and sat down with a couple of others in similar uniforms.

"That's Karl." Andrew told me. "Those guys he's with are Floor Service. Eh. Karl and I know each other from outside work too. He goes to some of the same clubs as me." He obviously doesn't rate your friendship quite as highly as you do Andrew, I thought. Either that, or he thinks you're too bloody mental.

We packed away our lunch trays, just like I used to do at school, and made our way back to the second floor for another round of mini-bar checking and filling.

Around 3 pm, Ahmet appeared in one of the rooms.

"Marco. Joe wants you upstairs with us to fill the new fridges on the 5th floor. You've probably spent more than enough time listening to this lazy gay-boy anyway."

I went upstairs and was reunited with the French duo of John-Mick and Didier. Joe was nowhere to be seen. Ahmet explained the deal. We had one of the huge mini-bar trolleys and a couple used by the maids – which were much smaller and pretty pointless for the job we had. The trolleys were being loaded up with stock from the store room downstairs, brought up to the floor and then we were to use those as a central supply to go into each room with a fridge starter pack of around 20 different mini bottles of various descriptions, four cans of soft drinks, a bag of peanuts and four glasses – two for wine and two tumblers. I realised on reaching the first fridge that the glasses only just fitted into the space needed for them and could see that would be a problem. I wondered if they would charge me for breakages.

I also realised on reaching the first fridge, that whilst I had been refilling fridges all morning, replacing missing items, that was a lot easier than putting everything in the right place into a virgin fridge. I had been filling in gaps, now I was looking into a void.

I grabbed one of the docket pads from the trolley and asked John-Mick if I could look in the fridge he had just filled. Five minutes later I had a sketch I could work from.

"That's good." John-Mick said, "Sort of thing a university student would think of." He gave me a knowing grin.

The Frenchmen and I carried on filling fridges until the end of the shift. John-Mick explained he was actually Jean-Mick. It hadn't occurred to me that John-Mick was a strange name for someone from Cannes. Jean-Mick, wasn't Jean-Michel. His mother was an anglophile and sneaked in the English spelling to make his name more exotic. Class. Obviously I had missed that his name wasn't John when Joe had introduced us. French wasn't one of his strong points, despite working with a lot of French waiters over the years.

Then Ahmet reappeared and asked if we could carry on working to get the fifth floor finished. That way we would be able to get the sixth filled over the next couple of days and we could all have a day off. There weren't any guests up there to get in the way.

Why not, I thought. Good to show willing and what else was there to do on a Sunday night. Overtime pay on Day 1? Get in!

By now Andrew rejoined us and I saw at first hand why he had infuriated Ahmet. Each room took him twice as long as the rest of us. I couldn't work out what he was doing, but his tics and twitches seemed to be getting stronger.

Booze in, cans in, nuts in, glasses in. Seal it, tick if off the list. Open the next room. Open the next fridge. do it all again.

It got towards nine o' clock and Joe made his first appearance of the day. I could smell cigarettes and alcohol on him. He seemed much lighter on his feet than he had been when I first met him this morning. He had a slight smirk in the corner of his mouth.

"OK boys? They been well behaved Ahmet? How many more have we got to do?" He was told just the end corridor Suite and one more room. Joe offered to do the Suite and Ahmet took the last room to show a bit of willing. Up to that point he had been 'supervising'. He didn't want to let his boss show him up after all. Bravo Joe and Ahmet - one fridge each. Set your team a good example why don't you. A taste of every manager I will ever come across in my future working life, I thought.

The rest of us slumped against one of the large trolleys. I was going to have to build some muscles and a whole load of stamina if I was going to last more than a couple of days in this job. I was also conscious of my stinking armpits. I'd kept my jacket on all day as I knew my shirt was going to be wet with sweat and I didn't want to have to put up with the rest of the team's horrified faces if I took my jacket off. Mind you they all smelt pretty bad too, apart from Andrew, who it seemed barely broke a sweat in anything he did.

"Are you OK Marcus?" Didier enquired. It was the first thing he had said to me all day. Earlier I had thought he was either very shy or English was beyond him. It turned out it was more to do with indifference to his surroundings and the people he worked with. He spoke excellent English, but his attitude was to do his job and not make friends.

Jean-Mick and Didier could not have been further apart as two Frenchmen if they tried. Both were in their late teens, like me. The Parisian Didier had the classic dark brooding looks and olive skin of a Film Noir actor. I imagined he smoked Gauloise and drank very small cups of coffees with the artists in Montparnasse. His 12 hour shadow had already gone full 24. I wondered what the guy in the Staff Department would say to him about shaving and bringing a razor to work. Didier had a slight frame, much thinner than Joe even, but the lad was very strong – he pulled the fully-laden trolleys up over the lip of the lift threshold as if he was adjusting a pram with a baby in it.

Jean-Mick on the other hand reminded me of Gerard Depardieu. Rotund features and stockier build. Like Didier and Andrew, he wasn't more than 5 foot 8. His sandy-blond hair sat on top of a very tanned face, with wide blue eyes and a even wider mouth, which seemed to be perpetually smiling. J-M offered open body language and seemingly took a genuine interest in finding out more about the world around him. I could see that I would get on with him more than the others. I suspected that most people would have said the same. It didn't surprise me when he told me his nickname at home was 'Mimo', after the sunny yellow flowers of the mimosa plants found on the Cote d'Azur.

The two of them didn't seem to get on particularly well together. I thought that as they were both from France, they would have shared heritage and what's more could use their language to bamboozle the rest of us. Although, to be fair, my O Level French would have allowed me to at least pick up who they may have been bitching about. I reckon I could have worked out what they were saying, given that I had developed a library of slang when I went on a school exchange trip at age 14. Indeed I could actually swear better in French than I could in English. Beyond that, I was always nervous about asking for the time, or for the way to the station, as I was always overcome with embarrassment about my terrible accent, which to this day is often mocked by my family.

Didier and J-M hardly spoke to each other in English, let alone in French. Whenever Didier did try his mother tongue on J-M, he would be rebuked in English. "You're here to learn to speak English. So use it you fucker", would be the reply. As I said, I liked Jean-Mick's style, even if Didier was already fluent and didn't need to learn anything.

I think much of the animosity came from the couple's backgrounds. Didier was an academic from Paris, whereas Jean-Mick had an English ex-model mother and a film maker for a father and had lived in Cannes all of his life. For him it was all about all about having fun driving his Fiat 500, or his micro-motorbike that he rode up and down Le Boulevard Anglais whilst whistling at any women who took his fancy. Unlike Didier, who spent his spare time in libraries, Jean-Mick lived on the beach and in the surf. Didier worked on his intellect, Jean-Mick on his tan. Didier was surrounded by books, J-M by girls. I had always fancied the idea of living in Paris, but now I was starting to think that life on the Med could well be a more interesting option.

Day 1 was over. I had gone from being verbally abused by the guy in the Staff Department to starting to discover the personalities of my work colleagues. I had found out what a mini-bar was and how to fill it. The work wasn't mind stretching, but the learning curve had been pretty damn steep.

Joe appeared from doing his one bar of the day. "OK guys. We finish filling the empty bars tomorrow. The 6th is a smaller floor and we can get that done with just two of you and Ahmet. The other two can check guest bars on the other floors. Take two floors each and whoever finishes first can do the 5th."

Andrew jumped in to ask if he could be put down to cover floors 3 and 4, which I learned later had less rooms than 1 and 2. Joe replied, "No you can do 1 and 2 as you are a lazy fucker, I'm going to give 3 and 4 to Marco. You up for it Marco?"

How could I refuse? I would be flying solo on day 2.

———

I got back to Dartmouth Rd at nearly 11.30 pm. I was totally knackered. Every muscle in my body ached. I would sleep like the dead that night, but knew I had to be up at 7 again to get into Bond Street for 8. I also had a haircut to do, having borrowed a pair of scissors from the Mini-Bar office. How difficult could that be? And I also better think about a shave too, although I would need to get a pack of razors first. Always helpful. I had never shaved using scissors before and wasn't about to try now.

There was a note left in the hall for me from Richard. *'Hi Dude. Came round to check if you did OK on your first day. I'm doing late shifts this week so won't be able to catch up until the weekend. Ciao, Richard.'*

Shifts? I wondered if that was heading my way too.

Day 2

The reality of shift patterns arrived when I got into work. Joe called us all to squeeze into the office where he held up an A4 piece of paper with undecipherable scrawl all over it.

"This is our shift pattern starting tomorrow. The hotel is open seven days a week and will be working three shifts, so that there is someone here most of the time. The morning shift is mainly to catch any bastard with an early check out. Reception will call you". Joe tapped the phone on the office desk. "And tell you that they have someone on front desk trying to leave."

He continued. "You run down the fire escape, as it's quicker than the lift, and get to their mini-bar. If they have taken anything overnight, you do a docket and put it into the terminal here. The day shift fills the bar later on their rounds. You've got to make sure the guest pays, or Accounts will be breathing down the back of my neck." I realised that 'making sure the guest pays' just meant generating a bill through the terminal. I didn't think we were expected to stop them in the street and demand they opened their wallets, although after yesterday, maybe we were.

The 'terminal' was literally a key pad with a hex-decimal display. All it needed was a three number room number followed by an amount, which required a full stop between pounds and pence. Forget that and you'd be charging 100 times too much and have the Accounts people jumping up and down on you and on more than your back.

"When the day shift starts, the early shift guy does one floor of rooms before they finish." So far it seemed sensible.

"If you are doing early shift you work from 6 am to 1 pm. You don't get a lunch. Before day shift starts, while you're waiting for the calls from Reception, you clean glasses in there." Joe pointed at the small silver metal service sink in the corner of the office.

He continued, "Room Service won't be in that early, so we can't use their machines. If you are caught asleep or reading porno I will have your bollocks."

Early shift didn't seem such a great option after all, although I did wonder what he meant about the porno.

"If you're on early on Sunday we will send a taxi to pick you up, so there are no excuses. Everyone can do it. If you have a hangover it needs to be gone by the time the taxi gets to the hotel. There's four of you, so you only have to come in the taxi once a month."

So far so clear.

"Day shift starts at 9 am and goes to 6 pm. You should be able to check two floors in that time, or maybe one and a bit if we're busy."

Or one, if you are Andrew, we all thought.

"Night shift is 3 pm to 11 pm. When you get in you should go to central stores to fill up our stock holding in the office, then do a floor if you have time, or help out the guys on day shift. After everyone else has fucked off, your job is also to clean glasses and wait for calls to be diverted from Reception or Floor Service, from people wanting stuff for their mini-bars after everyone else has gone home. Like the morning shift, sometimes people will check out in the evening and I want to make sure we bill them for everything they take."

"Me and Ahmet will be here on day shifts. Three days a week we will both be here. If you have holidays, we will change shifts about so that Ahmet covers a day shift. Before anyone complains about it, Ahmet has a wife and kid at home and lives outside London. He and me are also the fucking bosses, so we decide how it works. If you want to decide who works when, then you will have to get promoted. But I will have to leave first and I'm not going anywhere."

Management by dictatorship. None of Andrew's communist manifesto here.

I was going to point out that Joe's master-plan meant that each of us would be working a late followed by early shift at least once every two weeks, which must surely be illegal. By the time I'd get home I'd only have about four hours sleep before having to come back into work. So I asked him if there was a chance of staying in the hotel if we were to do a late then early shift.

"Marco. You are fucking joking me. Are you fucking calling me an asshole or something? I don't get to sleep here overnight and I'm the man in fucking charge. What do you want? Floor Service to come up and tuck you in? Fuck off Marco."

That would be a no then.

Joe's one concession was to allow us to swap shifts if we could agree it between us. This meant that as our days off in the pattern were spread out across the week, we could at least create the illusion of a weekend and put two days off together, if we could manage it.

Of course, no one wanted to swap their day shifts for early or lates and for some reason even swapping day shifts with Andrew and Didier was impossible. My only ally in trying to make space to see my family and Alison was Jean-Mick. He got it. He could tell I was still not much more than a child and I missed my Mummy and I really did have a broken heart.

— — — —

The rest of the day was uneventful. Doors open, fridge open, docket written, fridge filled, repeat. I had found the groove already.

Whilst easy work, it was tiring. The trolley weighed a ton and I was still getting to grips with the whole experience of doing more than lying in bed until lunchtime. On the upside, I was a working man. I could hold my head up high and show off my pay packet, when it finally came. I was doing an honest day's labour for an honest day's pay. I'd been sucked into Thatcher's dream of capitalistic man and I would work til I was muscle-bound, all day long.

At the end of the shift I decided I deserved a culinary treat. The only fast food back home was the local chip shop, miles away, so the riches available to me on every London high street were highly enticing. I found the nearest place to buy a burger, collapsed into a seat on the Jubilee Line and was soon in bed.

At least I knew I had a lie in ahead of me thanks to Joe's master plan. Hopefully I'd have enough time to do all those jobs that needed to be done before doing my first 'late'.

Day 3

I was going to be on my first late shift. Which was good news as I had stuff to do in the morning – like cut my hair and buy a razor, two jobs that I failed to do the day before. A bulky letter had arrived with a Gloucestershire postmark. My new address written on the outside in my Mum's handwriting.

Unfortunately the envelope had contained a selection of bars of chocolate, which had melted as the post was left on top of the hall radiator. Whilst the chocolate was ruined, at least the promised cheque was OK, even if there were a couple of brown smears on the back. Ann was more than pleased to receive the cheque when I knocked on her door on the other side of the staircase.

I then set about my haircut. I needed to go from on the shoulder to something that the guy in the Staff Department would deem an appropriate length. I decided that would be 'finger length'. If I put my left hand on my scalp then cut off anything coming out between my fingers that would be the right measurement. Seemed a good way to do it to me.

Ten minutes later I was picking up clumps of hair from the carpet of my room and congratulating myself on a job done, if not done well. I may be challenged by the Staff Department over incompetent self-inflicted hair cutting, but at least the length was OK and it was the length he had a problem with, wasn't it. The cut looked alright in the mirror too, even though I had no idea about the back of my head. I would just have to make sure I never turned my back on anyone important.

Next thing was shaving. Even though I was in my late teens, it wasn't something I did often, if at all, and my electric razor was still at home with all the other stuff I didn't expect I would need for a 'Weekend in London'. I had bought a pack of yellow and white Bic razors from the corner shop and went old-school shaving in the shared bathroom upstairs.

I don't know if it was the inferior tool, or the fact that I was shaving pretty much with cold water on a cold day using soap as shaving cream, but by the end of the session my face was covered in nicks and bits of wet toilet roll with dots of red blood that had seeped through. Anyone would think I had just walked onto the set of MASH as a shrapnel filled extra.

This was pretty grim, it looked like I had gone to get a haircut at Sweeney Todd's and he had decided to take my head off in the process. I pleaded with my face to stop bleeding and luckily for me by the time I got off the tube at Bond Street, most of it had. I wondered what my fellow passengers must have thought. 'Bleeding dickhead' was the expression that came to mind.

I rolled into the office where Ahmet was sat with his feet on the desk, day dreaming as he looked out of the window at the view of the fire escape and kitchen air-con units below.

"You alright Marco? Looks like there's something wrong with your head," he said as I seemingly woke him up. He was obviously referring to the haircut, or maybe my face full of fresh scars.

"Good news today. The French guys are working the floors, so they won't need any help, unlike that slow bastard Queen tribute act. Make us a cup of tea and let's have a chat."

Ahmet told me how he had grown up as a first generation Brit to Turkish Cypriot immigrant parents, but he was an East End lad, born and bred. On the other hand, whilst Joe had told me he was Maltese, he was actually originally from Cyprus. When Joe was a teenager, he had moved to Malta with his family after the Turkish army had invaded his part of the country.

Joe didn't like Turks - Mr P in Room Service was Turkish and there was a lot of bad blood between them. This could have been difficult for Ahmet, given that his family was from the wrong side of the island. But whilst Ahmet was Turkish by descent, he was English by birth, so it seemed Joe held no grudge against him. I suspect Joe just thought of Ahmet as a cockney geezer and had never asked him about his heritage.

The rest of the hotel workforce was from all over the world and apart from Andrew, the three Housekeepers and a guy in the Concierge team, I didn't meet another straightforward Englishman or woman in the time I was there. We were very cosmopolitan and Ahmet reckoned there were people from at least 50 countries who had all found a home in the Jupiter.

Ahmet told me how he had got married the year before at age 20 and now had a four-month-old daughter. I hadn't realised that he was only 21. He seemed a lot older when I first met him a couple of days before, mainly as he had told me that he had worked in Floor Service 'for years'. It turned out that meant two and not the four that I thought he had said. He would be waiting a while for a long service medal.

My Assistant Manager was a bit of a dreamer and told me about how he was planning to get out of Romford and move further East, maybe to the exotic up-and-coming towns of Braintree, Basildon. or Chelmsford. He even had an eye on

South Woodham Ferrers - which sounded less posh when he said it than it probably was in real life.

He didn't want his daughter growing up being scared of gangs and not knowing what trees looked like. He would also be a millionaire by the time he was 30 and would own a Ferrari. He picked up a picture frame from the desk, which had a very expensive looking sports car in it. "This will be mine by the time I'm 30." He said it with such conviction that I almost believed it myself. "One day you will walk past the hotel and see me and Joe driving past you in a red one. Don't shit yourself when you do."

When I asked him how he was going do that, he replied, "I got plans, Marco. I got plans." I suspected that he didn't. He mentioned that he had a brother with a kebab shop on Ilford High Street, who was doing well for himself, so maybe his plans involved mystery meat on a skewer. Ahmet had dreams, I'd give him that.

Jean-Mick broke into Ahmet's flow by coming into the office for some more docket pads. He seemed genuinely pleased to see me.

"Take a seat John", Ahmet instructed. He then continued to give us a long list of insights that would help us to navigate our lives in the hotel, or more importantly, how we would succeed as Fagin's urchins, working partly for the hotel, but mainly for him and Joe.

"Firstly, you have to understand that we work on a finder's keeper's basis." Ahmet said, putting this in air quotes for emphasis.

"If you want to keep anything you find in the rooms, after the guests have checked out of course, you have to run it by me first. I can tell you if it's rubbish and been left there on purpose, or if it's something of value that the guest may notice is missing and will want to come back for later. Strictly speaking you should give stuff like that to Security, who keep it for 30 days and give it to you if it's not claimed. But they sell the good stuff to a guy on Petticoat Lane, so you won't see it again. They'll tell you it was claimed by the owner, but you'll see it in the market a couple of weeks later."

"If you give stuff to me I will mind it for you and after 30 days you can either have it, or I will share it with you. Call it payment for my expenses and a thank you for keeping Security out of it. You get most of what you've found, which is a lot better than a whole lot of nothing."

I wondered what his expenses actually were in this process, but realised that asking that question wouldn't go down too well. It would be like Oliver Twist asking for more.

"Secondly, tips. The Floor Service guys are absolute fucking bastards when it comes to this. Guests often leave a bit of cash out as a tip for the staff. Unless there is a note on it that says, 'Thank you to the maid for making my bed and cleaning my room. Here is a tip', the first member of staff who gets into the room will trouser it. Joe didn't say it when he was talking about the late and early shifts yesterday, but he wants us to get to the rooms before anyone else does when a guest checks out. We have to make sure Floor Service doesn't get there before us, 'cause they will empty rooms of any good stuff – and the tips. A couple of them help themselves to the guests' tablets too, if they can find them. You need to keep out of their way when they've found a stash. It is amazing how aggressive a waiter can get when he's popped a few tranquilizers. You'll know who I'm talking about when you hear them rattling along the corridors looking like that Jack dude from The Shining."

I asked Ahmet about the maids and whether they did the same thing. I had visions of fighting over the contents of guests' rubbish bins and medicine cabinets.

"Don't worry about them. Joe has an understanding with the Housekeepers." He had put the word 'understanding' in imaginary speech marks too. "The Housekeepers manage the maids. You may have seen them at the other end of the corridor. There's a blonde, a brunette and a ginger one. I have to say that if I wasn't married, I would." Would what Ahmet, would what?

"Joe keeps them sweet, he always has done from his days in Floor Service. Where do you think he was when we were loading up the fifth floor the other day? He was in 624 with two of them, a bottle of vodka and a Do Not Disturb sign on the door. They look after the rooms so they can hide the evidence afterwards."

At this point my mouth must have been as wide open as Jean-Mick's smile. The penny had dropped, although it felt more like a 50p coin. Ahmet went on.

"Joe is a fucking randy bastard and I tell you what, I don't blame him. When he's on a shift with you and one of the Housekeepers says she wants to 'have a word' with him, you won't see him for an hour. And it's a lot more than a word he will be having with them. If you don't believe me go and have a listen outside 624."

"So what I'm trying to say is that it is up to us to screw the Floor Service guys by taking the tips that they want to steal from the maids. We are actually the good guys in all of this. We've agreed that if we find a tip under a pillow that we will give it to a maid if there is one nearby, otherwise you keep what you find - if the tip is on a table, that's fair game. But don't touch the drugs. Drugs are for those suckers from the first floor."

There were obviously official hotel rules, and the real rules that the staff had developed themselves.

"As I said, we're the good guys and the maids like us as a result. Floor Service? Nah, they are like the baddies in a bad Western. They don't give a shit about anyone else, so it's up to you to be the Sheriff and shoot them in their arses if you need to. If anything does ever go tits up, blame the Floor Service guys."

That was cryptic. I wondered what he was referring to. What could possibly go wrong when we were stealing the maids' tips and trying to empty rooms of anything of value that had been left by the guests, intentionally or otherwise? Ahmet continued.

"Joe has an understanding with the Housekeepers that as long as we don't take the piss, they will let us help ourselves and they get to carry on getting fucked by Joe as payment. Call it hush money. By the way lads, don't tell anyone about this outside of this room, not even to the other two, especially not Andrew."

I had to say at that point that I was just a little jealous of Joe. I had bumped into a couple of the Housekeepers in the lift on my way up and was stunned by them. They were sassy and super-confident. They knew that they were making me feel uncomfortable by the way I was blushing and trying to not look at anything apart from their eyes. After all I was just a naive, inexperienced country boy, who had never been that close to a 'real' woman before. They looked like they had walked out of a magazine.

Which led Ahmet on to his next point.

"Shift that box of Cokes will you John." Jean-Mick obliged and underneath was a pile of about 20 magazines. I could see straightaway what they were.

"That's our department porn collection. It's not much at the moment, as Joe and I only started here a few weeks ago, but I reckon that by Christmas it will be as high as you are Marco, you lanky streak of piss." Ahmet laughed at this in a way that made me hope that I hadn't found a new nickname.

"Again, I'm not going to talk to the other two about this because I don't think they would be interested. Andrew for sure. Didier maybe. What do you think John?" J-M shrugged and pushed his bottom lip out in the universal gesture of 'Who knows?'

"Where do we get this stuff from?" Ahmet asked, casually flicking through a 'Men Only' on the top of the pile. "From the rooms of course. This is what happens. Men on business come to London. They stop off at the newsagents opposite the hotel on the way in, or after they've checked in. We are a bit too far away from Soho for them to go there easily, and it's a scary place to hang out if you're from out of town. So they buy porn mags over the road and have a good hand shandy whilst waiting for Floor Service to bring them their dinner. One day hotels with put porn on the room TVs and the fat blokes in pin-striped suits won't need to bother with buying jazz mags."

"Of course they can't take their mags home to the wife, nor would they want to be found with them when going through customs, so the wankers leave them in their rooms. On a good day you may find 20 mags left lying about, having had only one careful owner. Your job is to bring any you find back here in your trolleys. Just make sure no one sees you stashing them. You wouldn't want to caught with a pile on you for obvious reasons."

My mind boggled. This was like a conversation 14-year-old lads would have had during a school camping trip.

"The stuff that's left is all legal, as I said they buy it from over the road. So we make a collection. Anything that is still current month, and is not covered in stains, Joe takes to the shop and sells it back to them for half price. The shop then sells it again to the next guest looking for something to keep them busy. The same mag can get sold four or five times. Call it recycling. Everyone is happy. That's why he lets you keep the tips you scrounge out of the rooms and I get a cut of the mag biz too."

"Any mags that are too tatty to resell, or are not the current month's, are yours to take. Good stuff gets added to the resale pile. If you have a look through what we've got in stock at the moment you'll see there are no October copies. Joe took them over the road yesterday."

"Why am I telling you this? Because at the end of each month we like to reduce our overhead and some of them get flogged to one or two of the porters and Mohammed in Floor Service. But Joe agreed that we would let you two have first pick before that. Just put your initials on any you want and you can have them when we sort out the pile each month. You should be able to maybe take 10 or 12 mags home each month, if you want them."

"We want you to work with us on this one. Bring us any porn you find in the rooms. If you do, you get to have a share at the end of the month and you also get to keep the tips. Fuck us over and start taking mags home and we will cut you off at your knees. By the way, you will need to think of a way to get the mags out of the building as Security sometimes does bag checks to make sure staff aren't nicking anything. You would not believe some of the shit that goes missing. A guy I used to work with in Floor Service has one of those massive round tables from Banqueting and ten of their chairs in his house, as well as ten full dining sets of knives and forks and even one of those fancy big candlesticks to go in the middle of the table. Just a shame he lives in a flat in Southwark."

"Oh yeah, I should have said, don't worry about Floor Service guys trying to muscle in on the porn business. They know Joe and I collect it, but don't know why. Most of them are gay and Mohammed is happy to pay for his supply. If you find any gay porn, just give it to Karl when you see him." I wondered if that was the same Karl who had ignored Andrew at lunch. He was obviously a collector of erotica, or had some side hustle going of his own.

"My next piece of advice is about Joe. If he tries to sell you anything tell him to fuck off. Joe doesn't sell stolen shit. He just sells shit. He knows people who import stuff from China. They load up a container over there and stick it on a boat to Tilbury. When it gets there Joe is waiting in his Capri, with a whole load of other Joe characters from other hotels. They do a deal with the guy at the dock to buy stuff off him. Joe then brings his shit home and stores it in his garage."

"You can tell when Joe has been to Tilbury, because the next day he will bring in a suitcase full of his Chinese imports. He'll give the Security guys a couple of bits of crap to get them to turn a blind eye to him lugging a suitcase through the staff entrance. If you want stuff that doesn't work, or is fake Rolex or Adidas, Joe is your man. I got some perfume off him once for my wife and it stank like cat piss when she put it on."

"Do not buy anything off him even if he says something like

'This 11 hour watch is just what you've been wanting Marco and it will make me very happy if you buy it'. He will look you in the eye in the same way as he looks at the Housekeepers when they want a word and before you know it he will have your cash and you will have a piece of crap. The only person getting fucked will be you. But otherwise he's a top bloke."

I asked Ahmet if he had ever spent any time with Joe out of work.

"It's a bit difficult. I'm married and have a kid. He just wants to go out and get pissed with his Greek and Maltese mates. Some of them know I'm Turkish, so they don't like me being there. We used to hang out before I was married, when I first joined the hotel. Ask him to tell you about the green pubes. I made the mistake of telling my missus about that story, so after that I couldn't really spend much time with him, even though the green pubes happened before I had met her."

Now, up to this point Ahmet's stories seemed reasonable and his advice useful. But a tale about green pubes as the reason why he and Joe had stopped drinking together had to be clarified and J-M made the request for further information before I did. I suspected Ahmet was itching to tell us anyway.

"OK you two. I'm only telling you this, because I don't want Joe to tell you first. It's one of those stories that you couldn't make up." I wondered how much of the rest of what he had told us was indeed fiction.

"Joe sometimes would come out to Romford to hear me DJ when I was about 18 and had just started here. It was kind of a big deal. For a lot of people in Romford, Joe was like a genuine mafia man. He would walk in and people would get out of the way. He'd be given bottles of Cristal and women would want to attach themselves to him. I kept telling people he was from

90

Malta, not Sicily, but nobody seemed to care. He got nicknamed Mafia Joe by the bar staff. Joe was the man!"

"I thought DJ'ing in the Romford and Ilford clubs were going to be a career step to bigger things, like some of the clubs in the West End. On a good night I could be playing my music to maybe 300 or 400 people, all pissed and getting into my tunes. I was hot property. You may have heard of 'DJ Kill-A'?"

Jean-Mick and I confirmed we hadn't. I assumed that was Ahmet's stage name.

"One night, when Joe was there, a really gorgeous girl came up to the DJ booth and started talking to me during songs. At that time this happened a lot, especially if a girl wanted a track played. Flirting was a way to get some airtime. And I liked to oblige. I was 18 and horny as hell after all."

"So this girl was talking to me and said she would show me her green pubes if I played her request. You know what those are don't you Marco?" He winked and smirked at Jean-Mick.

"I put on a long remix and went behind a speaker stack with her. She hitched up her skirt and I could see she had dyed her pubes green. Before anything else happened one of the bouncers walked past, so she pulled down her skirt and I tucked myself away. Nothing went off, except for me having a massive hard-on for the rest of the night."

"The next day at work, I was talking about what nearly happened. Joe calmly took out a matchbox, opened it and inside guess what was there? Some of her green pubes. I couldn't believe it!"

"Joe then said, 'Recognise these? I had sex with her that night in the car park. I couldn't stop laughing about her pubes, so she cut some off for me as a souvenir'. It felt like he was playing mind games with me and was trying to tell me who was boss, even when he was on my turf. I thought that was a pretty shitty thing to do to a mate, so decided to keep our relationship professional after that."

He continued his story.

"I have to say I did think twice about becoming his number two when this job was offered to me. But as I said, now I'm happily married and have my daughter. He is a sad old fuck that has no life, except some of the fantasy shit he gets up to in room 624. I don't think any of the Housekeepers are the same collar and cuff anyhow. I don't think any of them have the same colour and cuff and definitely not green, do you?"

I had no idea what that meant.

By this time Jean-Mick's shift had come to an end. He had only popped up for a pad of bill dockets, and two hours later was looking at a cup of cold tea with me next to him, having heard some stories about lives that I could not have imagined only a week ago.

I was left alone to do my late shift. That night I washed 76 glasses by hand and only took one call from someone in the kitchens looking for Joe. Did I have a look through Ahmet's pile of reading material? What do you think? Did I find the Housekeepers' photos in there? I'm pretty sure I did.

Day 4

My first day off and after last night I needed it. I got the last tube home from Bond Street and stumbled into bed about 1 am. There was a note left by Ann to say that she had paid the cheque in and that my mother had called 'for a chat' (I had given her Ann's number in case of emergencies). I would have to apologise for the interruption in the morning.

My first day off in London as a working man with nothing much to do. Richard had already told me how he wasted a lot of time building up a mental map of parts of London by walking around them. OK, I decided to do the same thing.

Where did I know in London? Our family used to make an annual trip when I was a kid to go to the odd sightseeing spot, such as feeding the pigeons in Trafalgar Square, looking at Big Ben, going around the Tower of London and other touristy bits. Mum used to collect vouchers on soap boxes that paid for the train tickets and the rest of the day would revolve around a big tote bag of packed lunches. I knew the underground tunnel from South Ken tube to the museums pretty well and still remained convinced that the underpass was the inspiration for Dr Who's Cybermen. Apart from the Museums in South Ken and a tiny bit around Charing Cross, there was a whole city I had no idea about.

Carnaby Street. That's a place I hadn't been to before. I would go there.

But first I wanted to write a long letter and a short letter. The long letter was to Alison in Leeds to tell her some of the details of my first few hours in London and how much I missed seeing her, as we'd been pretty much inseparable during the last year and a half at school.

The short letter was to my Mum and Dad thanking them for the cheque which had arrived safely and sorry not to have called, but I was very busy with work. And by the way, don't call that number unless it really is an emergency, as it was in my landlady's part of the house. I would save some 10ps and call them soon.

Letters posted, I got on the tube and alighted at the now familiar Bond Street. From there I walked along Oxford Street, electing to walk in the road with the buses and taxis, as this seemed a lot safer than taking my chances with the meandering tourists. I turned right at Oxford Circus and headed down Regent Street past many huge shop fronts and shortly I could see the Tudor beams of the Liberty shop at the end of Carnaby Street.

Now, my expectations of this place had been formed from a mixture of late 60's record sleeves, especially Hendrix, and some of the photos of The Beatles and the Stones taken about the same time. I was anticipating loons in loons with flowers in their hair. Bell-bottomed flared trousers, patchouli and rainbows. Instead it was a mixture of overpriced vintage clothes shops and tourist emporia where you could buy anything your heart desired, so long as it had 'Carnaby St, London W1' embossed on it.

The vintage shops were a particular let-down. I did manage to find a red Hendrix-style guardsman jacket – for £150 - and a whole load of stuff that I was sure I'd seen in the Army and Navy Surplus back home for less than a quarter of the price. Rip the tourists off by all means. But what about us Londoners? Of course no Londoner would shop on Carnaby St, it was just that I had no idea where else to go.

On my way back to the tube station, there was a man selling hats from a makeshift stall covered in plastic sheeting. On it was one very similar to the one Didier had been wearing a couple of days before. I had no idea what to call it but it reminded me of Humphrey Bogart. It was gray and had a black band around it, which was crying out for a pheasant feather to be stuck in it. Every man should have a signature hat and this looked like it could be mine.

I have a particularly large head and finding hats to fit is always difficult. But the trader assured me that it would expand with wear and that I'd be getting a bargain. Failing that, all I needed to do was make a cut in the lining. Simple.

Having just got some money out of the bank I decided to waste £20 of it on the hat. I was celebrating being in London and I thought I probably looked the dog's bollocks as I got back on the tube. With hindsight, I just resembled an extra from an Ealing Comedy. All I needed was a mackintosh, a rolled up an umbrella and a black and white filter.

Later that afternoon, I tried calling Richard at Mr Biddle's on the off chance he was there. He was. Like me, it was his day off too. He suggested that we walked from his digs to Westfield College, which was just down the Finchley Road. One of our friends from school, Judy, was two months into her degree course there and he was sure she would love to see us both.

I hung up and went to West Hampstead on the tube, then took the short walk past the 1930's houses of Sumatra Road, to where Richard was living. Complete with hat I knocked on Mr Biddle's door.

Richard greeted me with a guffaw. "I don't get it. Why, just why?" I told him that we all needed a style and that I was sure that he would be buying one too, in the same way as I had copied his blue/gray Kicker shoes by buying an identical pair, although mine were gray/blue. (I should have also admitted to having copied his cord jacket, granddad shirt and navy blue greatcoat too. But he had copied most of that from his older brother and Hendrix in the first place).

We started strolling. Richard told me that his relationship with Buddle was getting quite bad. He had agreed to pay him £75 a month to cover bills and make a contribution towards some of the food he was eating. But it had been his girlfriend Harriet's birthday yesterday and that had cost a bit. And he also bought a new acoustic guitar in Greek Street at the weekend. Of course when Buddle heard him playing that he wanted to know how Richard had the money for the guitar, but not for rent.

I asked him how much he owed.

"Well, you know I moved to London at the end of July?" I nodded. "Since then really." So four months, or three and a bit if we were being generous with the basis of calculation. It didn't need much adding up. He owed a lot.

"Yes, it's about £350 at the moment", Richard confessed. "I just don't know where my money goes. Living in London is fucking expensive man." I couldn't see how staying at Mr Biddle's would be sustainable. And if not, what was he going to do about it?

"My biggest fear is that he is one of my brother's lecturers. He's going to tell him what's going on and Charles will report back to my parents. They already think I'm dossing about in London and should be doing something worthwhile before I go to Sussex next year. Buddle won't kick me out though. I reckon he's tried it on with Charles. Charles isn't gay, but he's a bit of a liability. There must be something like that stopping Buddle. If there is, then I shall carry on living rent free for as long as possible." It was a strategy, but a high risk one and one that was most certainly unsustainable.

We walked up a rainy hill to the Westfield campus, a brutalist concrete block that looked very out of place in comparison to the rest of the red brick and whitewashed mansions surrounding it.

Any ideas how to find Judy? "Let's try the Students Union", Richard suggested. At this point I had probably spent less than an hour in a university, apart from a couple of set piece open days I went to as part of my failed UCAS application. Imposter syndrome set in.

The Union bar was full of people wearing duffle coats and the Westfield colour scarf. I had thought that was the stuff of stories. Surely people don't wear those in real life? At the far end of the bar was a familiar mop of curly blonde hair.

"Richard! Marcus. What are you two doing here? And why are you wearing that hat?", Judy spluttered. Richard explained that he lived in the neighbourhood and we thought we would pop in to have a beer with our old friend from school and see how it was going.

He then confessed to not having any money in his pocket and I made some excuse about leaving my wallet at home. I had it in my pocket, but it was empty. So Judy suggested we went back to her room in the Halls of Residence to continue to talk there. She still had a bottle of wine that her parents had left with her when she moved in. "Don't mind if I do", replied Richard.

Her room was the standard student space: a tiny single bed with shelving over it; a table; a desk; and a small wardrobe. Judy had put an Indian scarf over the bedside table, which had the effect of making the room gloomy. Indian stuff was very popular among the hippies that inhabited our home town and I suspected it had come from there. The first impression of the student experience wasn't great. Be a student and live in a chicken coop.

Richard unloaded his tale of woe about his uncaring landlord. I chipped in with the odd comment about my strange conversation with Ahmet earlier in the day, but Richard was holding court and the less wine there was left in the bottle, the more he spoke.

About an hour in I realised that neither of us had asked Judy about her time at Westfield. She gave a short summary of her languages course content, spoke about some of the great mates she had made, suggested that the people we knew back home were all a bit flaky and dull and talked about a gig she had been to the night before. A band called Echo and The Bunnymen. With a name like that I said I would check them out, after all Richard and I were still listening to Hendrix and Steely Dan and other prog rock bands. It was time for something different.

Shortly afterwards, Judy told us that she had a seminar to prep for and that she would see us about. I hopped on the tube at Swiss Cottage as Richard said he would walk back to his. Not a single person laughed at my hat on the way home. Maybe it wasn't so crap after all.

Day 5

When I got home I was absolutely freezing cold. The house lacked central heating, so I put the two-bar electric fire on in the same way I had the night before. I didn't think anything of leaving it on overnight. It made the room toasty and gave it a pleasant orange glow. I suppose I could have put on another blanket, but I had never had to think about that sort of thing at home. Heat just happened.

As I left the house to head off on a day shift, Ann jumped out of her doorway sporting a dressing gown. It looked like she had literally just got out of bed.

"Marcus. Have you been using your fire all night?" she said in her almost indecipherable accent. I contemplated lying. What interest was it to her? Maybe I was spending too much time with Richard, and was tempted to make the denial. But I felt rumbled and embarrassed, so I confessed that I had, and asked her what the problem was.

"It burns too much electric. I've been watching the dial on the meter. When you came in last night it started to go so much faster. My husband wanted to break your door down and get you to turn it off." Which was interesting for two reasons. Firstly I hadn't considered the price of electricity before – I just plugged stuff in and turned things on - and secondly, I hadn't realised there was a Mr Ann. I also wondered why he wanted to kick the door in when she had a spare key?

I apologised and told her it wouldn't happen again. She asked me if I needed more blankets. I accepted the offer, knowing that they would not be as warm as the fire, but would have to do. She disappeared into her doorway under the stairs and reappeared a couple of minutes later with two beige, very thin blankets, that I squirreled away into my room.

— — — —

The morning at work was relatively uneventful. I checked most of two floors and didn't find any porn, nor any tips. Maybe Ahmet had made all that up as a joke at my expense.

Lunch was interesting. I was sat with Didier eating some form of 'meat pie', that had been unspecified on the blackboard menu.

Across from me was Mohammed, the guy from Floor Service who Ahmet had said he supplied porn to on a monthly basis. The conversation was stilted and at some point Didier compared something I said about the mysterious meat pie to the 'Chicken and Egg situation'. Mohammed jumped at him and wanted to know what he meant. Didier gave him a sly smile in the corner of his mouth and slowly raised an eyebrow. "Hey Mohammed, it's not a problem. Is just a chicken and an egg. Which was the first? Everything comes from eggs. Egg before chicken."

Mohammed was enraged. He shouted at Didier that it was the chicken that must have been first, how else could the egg have been laid? He should know that Allah created all of the living creatures first, not the eggs. Was Didier mad or something?

Didier's mother tongue being French and Mohammed's Arabic, the two of them were bound to have some misunderstandings when talking about philosophy in English. But Mohammed now had his knife raised above his head and Didier was hiding behind my chair. I doubt that Plutarch had this in mind when he posed the question back in ancient times.

For a moment, I thought fucking hell. I've been here less than a week and I'm about to get stabbed by an Algerian who wants to actually kill a Frenchman because he said the chicken came first. I wanted to do a degree in biology when I eventually sorted my life out, but this was taking the argument of evolutionary theory a bit too far. I didn't want to be dissected either. Luckily, a couple of the porters grabbed Mohammed's arms and sat him at a different table with a couple of gentle slaps on his cheeks to calm him down.

Everyone else just carried on eating as if nothing had happened.

It was only on the way out of the canteen that I realised the meat in the pie was chicken. But I wasn't going to tell Mohammed that.

As I said, pretty uneventful. The Staff Department guy did come upstairs to ask Didier what had gone on at lunchtime and Didier calmly told him he didn't know what he was talking about. Of course, I didn't know he had said that. When I was questioned later as a witness, I too played it down as nothing much, although I did mention that there had been a disagreement about the contents of a chicken pie. Mini-Bars hated Floor Service (of which Mohammed was one) and Floor Service hated Mini-Bars. But we both hated the Staff department even more.

———

As this was my first day shift, after I'd checked and filled my two floors, Ahmet gave me a couple of trays of dirty glasses and told me to take them down to the Floor Service office on the first floor. Ahmet assured me that Floor Service had a dishwasher who could do them in half the time it would take me to do them in the office sink.

I strode confidently into the large Floor Service room, full of equipment and piles of crates and boxes. Despite being nervous, I was walking into enemy territory and I didn't want the opposition to smell the fear, given that I was nearly stabbed by one of them at lunchtime.

A round, overweight man in his late 50s, dressed in a morning suit, stopped me after a couple of paces.

"Who da fuck are you?" he asked. I told him I was Marco, I worked with Joe and I was looking for the dishwasher to do these glasses.

It was my first encounter with the infamous Mr P, enemy of the people.

"Is over there." He pointed towards the back of the gloomy workspace, past a couple of Floor Service waiters who were huddled over an ashtray.

The rest of the floor space was full of dirty trays piled high on wheeled trolleys. I had to negotiate a pathway, holding two crates of 36 glasses at the same time. The two guys weren't going to help me. I was Mini-Bars after all.

I pushed the trolleys out of the way with my hips and put the glasses on a table at the far side of the room. I turned back round to Mr P and called over, in a rather timorous voice, to ask where the dishwasher was. Was he on a break, and what time would he be back?

"You a fucking idiot or something?" Mr P replied, shouting over the noise of the two waiters pissing themselves laughing. "Is not a man, is a machine and you are resting on him."

OK. Now this was embarrassing. I had assumed that the dishwasher was a human being who was destined to lurk at the back of Floor Service spending his days cleaning our glasses. I felt like a schmuk. So instead of a man I was faced with a machine.

Having never had the opportunity to operate an industrial-size dishwasher before, nor having seen a domestic one in situ either, I was baffled. It looked like the trays of glasses must go on a conveyor belt and be sucked through it somehow. There was a lever that seemed to operate a door and an on-off button over which someone had written 'Do not use.'

I put the glasses on the conveyor belt and still nothing came to life.

"Hey Karl, show the Mini-Bar idiot how to use the dish-washer", Mr P shouted, frustrated by the incompetent stranger in his department.

Karl came over from where he had been smoking. He looked like a more agreeable version of Andrew; he certainly had teeth, even if they may not have been his own. I realised he was the waiter whose attention Andrew was desperate to attract during our first lunch and that he was also the suspected collector of gay porn that Ahmet had joked about when giving us the Oliver Twist briefing.

Karl calmly took the trays and shoved them in the machine. "Look, lower the door here. Turn it on at the wall. Always helps to push the button. I know it says do not use. That's just a joke, because no one here can be arsed to clean up after themselves.

You see these trays of dirty plates?" He pointed at a pile of about 15 breakfast trays full of the remains of that morning's deliveries. "Enough said."

Two minutes later I had two trays of steaming clean glasses on the conveyor belt ready to take back to the 6th floor. I thanked Karl for helping – he was one of the first people I had met in the hotel who had actually been kind.

The phone rang and Mr P yelled across the room, "Karl. Is your wife!"

I returned to the office to find Ahmet looking a bit annoyed about something.

"What went on downstairs? Were you taking the piss out of Mr P? Why did you tell him you thought there would be a man there to clean the glasses? Floor Service fucking hate us and now they hate us even more. They think you are a dickhead Marco.......Did you get the glasses cleaned?"

I assumed that Ahmet had taken a phone call from Mr P the moment I left the Floor Service space. I could imagine that it wouldn't have been too friendly.

"Joe has gone to sort this with Mr P, as he's said he doesn't want any 'Mini-fucking-Bar fucking idiot fuck-ups fucking about with our fucking dishwasher' in his Floor Service space any more. In other words, we're banned from using his machine and from now on it will all have to be hand jobs up here. I hope you like washing dirty glasses cos you and them are going to spend a lot of time together. All this shit is down to you, Marco."

I apologised profusely. I realised that I had indeed fucked up. It hadn't been deliberate, I had honestly expected to find a bloke in a uniform who had the job of washing up. It was just a shame that it was the first time I had met Mr P, and without realising it, I had crossed swords with him. I suggested to Ahmet that he spoke to Karl about it. Karl had helped me and he seemed a reasonable bloke. He would tell Joe and Ahmet what really happened. I hadn't been rude nor aggressive, I just misunderstood the task.

"Karl's probably after your arse. You're the new boy in town. He's always on the hunt for fresh meat." I was confused. I said to Ahmet that he just couldn't be gay, he has a wife for Chrisssake. Mr P had even taken a call from her when I was down there.

Ahmet started laughing and asked me to say what I had just said again, just as a rather perplexed Joe walked into the room.

"Hey Joe, listen to this. Before you go off on one about the dishwasher, listen to this. Say it again, Marco." I repeated what I heard. Karl wasn't gay because he had a wife.

Joe rolled his eyes. "That's not a woman you fucking idiot Marco. That's his boyfriend they were talking about. Karl is the most gay man in the whole of the hotel and that is saying a lot, as apart from Mohammed, that whole department are a bunch of queers. Mr P only hires them – me and Mohammed were there before he turned up, and when he met Ahmet he thought Ahmet was bent because of his gay haircut. He wouldn't have been hired if Mr P knew the truth. I think Karl is possibly the most gay waiter of every hotel in London. If Karl asks you to go out for a beer with him, make sure you don't turn your back on him." For a moment I thought he was talking about my terrible haircut and how I should avoid showing it.*

The effect of my mistake about Karl's sexuality had diffused any anger that Joe may have brought upstairs after talking about my dishwasher experience with his old boss. Joe sat on the edge of the desk, folded his arms and pursed his lips.

"You know what Marco? I say fuck Mr P. I would have loved to have seen his face when he thought you were taking the piss by asking what time the dishwasher started work. I'll get us our own machine - and hand washing gets the glasses cleaner anyway. But do me a favour, don't go back into Floor Service again and if you see Mr P in a corridor, get into the nearest room, or he will have your bollocks. He's a fat old bastard, but he has a lot of power in this hotel. He's not a good man to have as an enemy."

As I said, a pretty uneventful day.

On my way home I popped into the HMV megastore just along from Bond Street. The largest HMV in the world, sprawling over five floors. I went to the tape section and looked for the Es. There it was: Echo and the Bunnymen. Let's start with 'Crocodiles'. All I needed now was my tape deck from home.

— — — —

Footnote

*I had not really been exposed to homosexuality before. Despite being at an all boys' school. True, we did used to joke about certain boys who had a feminine air about them and sing "Girls mean nothing to he" to the tune of Ultravox's Vienna as they walked past.

One lad, Austin, came out in the 4th year, but we thought he was joking to start with. He was from a traveller community and had a tough time of it at home, ending up in hospital as a result of telling his family about his feelings. I used to sit next to him in my English lessons and he was a good mate. I didn't try to understand what he was going through, which I regret to this day. I hope he found a way to be happy.

Boys used to play at being gay too. Or at least we thought they were. The advice was never play in the front row of the scrum if Stephen Dewsbury was in the second row - unless you wanted your balls felt by him. We were all reluctant to go in the showers after games, mainly as it meant being ogled by the teachers and if 'Dewey' was there forming a one boy audience, washing was not an option. It was his 'thing'. Some people were known for being in bands, others were train-spotters, some were into football, Dewey was the school perve.

The drummer and bass player from Richard's band, Eddie and Martin, would also put on a show before school started in the Lower 6th Common room simulating sex on the teacher's desk. All in the name of shock and awe. I remember it as embarrassing rather than erotic.

It was surprising that there were not more obvious expressions of sexuality, given there were over 800 boys in the school, and some dodgy teachers too - at least one of which is now behind bars. I suppose this was the late 70s/early 80s. Boy crushes on cool kids were more about being part of their fan clubs than wanting to get naked with them and if anything was going on, it was kept very, very secret.

Day 6

My first morning shift. Getting out of bed at 5 am was difficult enough. Having a cold bath in two inches of water, worse. Another unsatisfactory shave and the realisation that none of my shirts smelt of anything other than sweat. A few moments later they smelt of sweat and Lynx. It would have to do until I could get some washing done.

OK. Early morning on Willesden Green tube station, watching the mice running across the tracks, and studying the film posters on the walls of the waiting room building. 'Rocky III', 'Gandhi' and 'An Officer and a Gentleman' all cried out for attention. I wondered if I should invite them all round for a fictional dinner party/boxing match. It would be interesting, although I couldn't work out if the officer and the gentlemen were one or two people. I was still half asleep and wishing I was in bed.

I picked up the office keys from the guy on the security desk after clocking in, signing my name underneath Didier's who had been on the late shift the day before and had handed them back close to midnight.

How hard could a morning shift be? A chance to sit and wait for the rest of the hotel to come in. I poured some hot water from the office kettle into a cup with instant coffee in it. I would need a lot of these today.

At 6.30 am the phone rang. It was Reception: "I need a mini-bar check for 223." I grabbed my docket pad, locked the office door and headed down the fire escape two steps at a time until the number 2 appeared next to a doorway onto the floor.

229. 227. 225. 223. Hello, Mini-Bars! Silence. I opened the door and went in.

The room was relatively tidy, just the bed-sheets pulled on to the floor. This guest must have been in late and left early. Check the bins and bathroom for porn, take a piss in the toilet. Have a look at the mini-bar. The seal hadn't been broken, so no action needed. Quick call to Reception on the room phone to say there was no billing due and the guest was released from the front desk.

Five minutes later I was in the office when the phone rang again. "Mini-bar check for 412." Only two floors down this time. Look under the pillow for tips (I'd forgotten that first time), check the bins for porn, check the mini-bar. The seal was broken, but nothing appeared to have been touched inside. I looked on the bedside table and noticed a litre bottle of Jim Beam with just under half still in it. Well that will go down well with Joe and Ahmet when they come in later, I thought. Call to Reception to tell them the room was clear. No need to mention the Jim Beam to them.

Fortunately, room 412 was next door to the fire escape, so no one would notice me sneaking back to the office with half a litre of whiskey in my hand. Not a good look before 7 am.

Another ten minute gap and then a call to tell me there were three rooms checking out at the same time. Why do people always want to check out on the hour? So some nimble footwork between floors to find three untouched mini-bars but a couple of magazines for Joe's side hustle. I glanced inside them on the way back to the office. I was out of breath from running up and down stairs, or that's what I told myself.

Another five calls from Reception before the day shift arrived. All but one hadn't touched their mini-bars. I started to wonder if people knew what they were. After all, had you gone to any London hotel a year before, you wouldn't have found a mini-bar in your room. Like all things that seemed a luxury to start with, they were now becoming commonplace, but our guests seemed to be old school. They could just about work out how to use the kettle in their rooms and find the Floor Service number on their phones for everything else.

Of those five calls, no porn, two lots of tips (61p and 80p) and not a lot else. Except the cigars.

I got called down to a smaller room on the second floor at about 7.20 am. The room was empty except for a tray with the remains of last night's delivered dinner. A cigar box, the size of a shoe box, was placed on the desk in front of the large wall mirror, used by the guests to see what they looked like dressed... and sometimes to see what other guests looked like undressed.

I thought, fuck - is this a bomb? The IRA had been blowing bits of London up for the last few years, and I had learned in the canteen the day before that there had been a terrorist attack on an El-Al flight crew at the hotel in 1978. A flight attendant was killed, nine were wounded and one of the Palestinian terrorists died too. The terrorists used grenades and machine guns on the crew as they left the hotel to get on a bus to go to Heathrow. You could still see two dents in the door frame where bullets had hit it.

So there I was looking at a closed box of Havana cigars, admiring the pastel painted picture of a couple embracing on a Hispanic balcony, with 'Romeo y Julietta' inscribed above the image. I was sure I had seen an episode of Colombo when a bomb was put in a cigar box. Or was it exploding cigars that killed people? Who knew. Exploding cigars? That was probably from a Laurel and Hardy film. I needed to focus.

After a couple of minutes considering how much explosive would be needed to kill me, I decided there was only one thing for it - open it. I suspected it would be empty anyway.

I weighed up the best way to flip the lid off the box. Maybe if I crouched down under the table it would save me from most of the blast, if that was what I had in store. So I moved the chair and got down in the foot-well of the desk. My right hand gingerly moved towards the lid, fingers shaking, heart racing.

I had a sudden thought. If it does blow, I'm definitely going to lose my hand, so I switched position so that I would waving goodbye to my less useful leftie.

I flipped the lid and closed my eyes and paused for a couple of seconds in case it had a timer on it. Nothing exploded. I was not dead and at the last count I still had a full set of fingers.

OK. So what had I found? Imagine my surprise when I stood up to see a box that was supposed to hold 50 Cuban cigars that still had 48 cellophane wrapped smokes in it. I punched the air. This was surely better than a porn mag, even though I didn't smoke. The bosses will like this one, a lot.

I grabbed a napkin from the breakfast tray, wrapped the cigar box in it and scurried back to the office with my find.

Shortly after 9 am Ahmet appeared. It was his day to keep an eye on us scruffy bastards.

"How was the morning? Busy?", he enquired. Obviously

I had no benchmark. Had it been busy, or was it relatively quiet? I didn't get much time to drink coffee and the only radio I managed to listen to was when I was in the empty rooms making out the dockets. I now knew that a mini-bar check lasts about half a regular pop song on Radio 1.

"Get any goodies?" Ahmet asked eagerly, in the same way as Fagin would have asked his boys. I had an image of Ahmet in finger-less gloves rubbing his hands together in anticipation. I showed him the two porn mags, which he wasn't that impressed with, mainly as we were heading towards the end of the month and he knew the window for resale was getting narrow.

Then I told him to shut his eyes and when he opened them the cigar box was on the desk in front of him. I explained what I had to do to open it and told him that this must surely be the mother of all stuff found in rooms. 48 Cuban cigars.

Ahmet's face lit up. "Shit. This is one hell of a find. Thank fuck that you got to it before Floor Service. Have you any idea what these are worth? No, me neither, but my uncle smokes cigars and I know he spends about £20 on a good Cuban. That's nearly ten grand's worth in here. Ten grand! You and me are in the money my son. Have I done the maths right?"

He got out a calculator. "48 times 20 quid. That's 960 quid. Fuck me. That's still a lot of dosh. Drinks on you my boy Marco."

I put the kettle on, it was way too early to crack open a champagne, or the whiskey bottle found first thing in the morning.

Ahmet looked agitated. "Now. Hang on. What time did Reception call you on this one? Sometimes a guest checks out after they finish their breakfast and then goes to collect their stuff before leaving the hotel. Germans do that a lot. Was it a German in the room? What else was left in there? Were there any cases or clothes lying about. Did you see a toothbrush or anything else in the bathroom?" I assured him the room was totally empty apart from the cigar box and the remains of a breakfast tray.

"Well Marco my friend. I really should hand this one into Security. There's a good chance that the guest will come back for it, or call the hotel and ask to have it sent on when they realise that they have left a year's supply of cigars in their room. Security will hang on to it for 30 days, and if it isn't claimed then they should give it back to you."

I nodded and confirmed that was indeed hotel policy.

"Only they won't. I can tell you for a fact that you will go down there after 30 days and they will tell you the cigars were claimed by their owner. Then every time you leave the building one of them will be outside with one of our cigars in their mouth. There's no way we're going to let that happen."

He was echoing his security brief from a couple of days before.

Ahmet's plan was to keep the find between him and me. Joe didn't need to know about this and I wasn't to talk to the other lads about it. The more people who knew about it, the more people would have to take a share. Ahmet would hide the box and when we felt it was unlikely that anyone would claim them, we could take them home.

Of course, if the guest got in touch and wanted the cigars back, and Security wanted to find out why they hadn't been handed in, we would just say that Floor Service must have got to the room first, even though they didn't open their department for another hour and a half. Security were quite scared of Mr P anyway, so their investigation would more than likely close if we directed them to him. They didn't like to accuse any of his boys of being thieves, even though they knew that they were all probably thieves on an industrial scale.

Ahmet told me that he would take a couple home as samples, to get his uncle to price them for us. He took five out of the top of the box and then asked me to stash it on the highest shelf behind a case of Cointreau.

A couple of days later, Ahmet would inform me that his uncle reckoned that the cigars would cost about £12 each from his supplier. Which still made a very tidy sum. "So we split the box in a couple of weeks, yeah? 43 cigars divided by two. Call it 20 for you and the rest to me."

I didn't have the energy to argue about the extra cigars that he'd already taken as samples, half of which were strictly speaking mine.

What was I going to do with nearly £250 worth of cigars anyway? Except maybe stick them in my friends' jacket pockets when I saw them back home down the pub at Christmas. Yeah that sounded good. 'So you're enjoying Uni? I'm working in London now, and I'm a big fucking deal - here, have a cigar. Yes, they are real Cubans - just like the ones that Castro smokes'. The image of a load of teenagers puffing on cigars at our local is something I had to look forward to.

That Christmas Eve at The Lodge later became known as 'Cubana Night'. The locals were confused both by the over-rich aroma from the fug the cigars created and by the student punters smoking Cuba's finest. That evening was the stuff of legend and will be remembered for a lot of puking kids in the outside bogs, who couldn't handle the strength of the thigh rolled tobacco.

I was buzzing from the cigars for the rest of my shift. So much so that I nearly made a major mistake.

— — — —

One of the suites on the third floor was a late checkout and the guest was being allowed to leave at lunchtime. I was due to go home, although I was planning to sneak into the canteen and have something to eat before I did. Strictly speaking we weren't allowed to do that. The rule was one meal per shift and I had already grabbed some eggs on toast when the day shift started.

Ahmet grabbed me as I picked up my coat. "Do me a favour Marco. 301 is a late checkout. Can you get down there and check the mini-bar? One of the housekeepers said it's a famous opera singer. You like music don't you? If she is still in her room get her to give you a song."

I thought, I'm at the end of a shift, but OK. I took the lift. At the fourth floor Andrew got in with his trolley. We exchanged the usual 'Busy? Yes, busy' pleasantries and he got out with me on the third. The lift cable seemed to have stretched even more than usual.

301 was a suite. It was an empty suite. Unsurprisingly there was no porn to be seen, but there was a £5 note under the pillow. Maybe I would let this one go to the maid who was in the room next door. I looked in the mini-bar – just a bottle of water had gone. Then I noticed a massive bouquet of white flowers propped up against the wardrobe. Wow, what an impressive display. Someone must really love the woman who had been in the room that night and these certainly hadn't been delivered by Interflora.

I thought, hey why not? The office could do with brightening up a bit. So I returned via the fire escape this time, bumping into Mohammed on the way. His only comment was, "Nice flowers", instead of "Why are you carrying half a florists' up a fire escape?"

I walked into the office to announce that it was just a bottle of water gone and hey look what I found. The display was now a little battered from being knocked on door frames, but remained impressive none the less.

Ahmet keyed the room number and the price of the bottle into the accounts terminal. His olive face turned white like the lilies I was now proudly sticking in the office sink in an effort to re-hydrate them.

"Marco. What room did I send you to?" 301 I confirmed.

"Fuck, that guest hasn't checked out yet. You've just stolen the fucking bouquet she probably got after singing at the Royal Albert last night."

OMG, what was I going to do. One minute I was patting myself on the back for the discovery of Fidel's finest, and now I was going to probably get arrested for flower theft.

Ahmet said. "We have to take them back. If anyone asks what the fuck we are doing, leave it to me. I don't know what I will say, but I will think of something. You just shut your mouth and carry those flowers back downstairs."

We opened the fire escape door. The smell of lunch filled our nostrils. If you were to go down 14 flights of stairs you would find yourself in the basement by the kitchens. Staff were not supposed to go on the emergency stairs between 12.30 and 2 pm, as each time we opened the doors to the fire escape, the whiff of whatever muck the staff were having for lunch would creep onto the floors.

From experience, and the fact that the 'no fire escape' rule was in the main ignored, those aromas not only permeated the air on the guest floors, but they lingered too. A few times I was asked by Americans what the smell was and I used the same line that all of the staff used, namely that we couldn't smell it. It was particularly bad when roast potatoes or cabbage were involved.

My nose didn't have time to work out what we were having for lunch. It was buried in the pollen from the flowers that I was now clutching to my chest, in a vague attempt to stop them getting damaged further. My jacket would have yellow pollen streaks on the lapels for the remainder of the time I wore it as a result. It just added to the idea that Mini-Bars were by far the scruffiest group of employees in the building. A medal we continued to wear with honour, although my lapel badge was made of nectar and pollen.

We arrived at the third floor entrance. Fortunately no one else had been on the stairs. Ahmet told me to wait there. He would go into the room to check it was empty. I could see him through the reinforced glazed panel in the fire door. He knocked on the door, called 'mini-bars!' and then came back to me. "I've not got a fucking key. But I don't think there's anyone in there. At least, no one came to the door or called back."

I scuttled across the corridor hoping that no one would notice me. After all I was just a bloke with a massive bunch of flowers, and there's nothing wrong with that.

After the third attempt my door key worked and we slipped inside the suite. Ahmet gestured for me to wait by the door and he darted in and out of the rooms and hall to check if there was any sign of life. He whistled for me to come forward.

"Where did you find them?" I pointed, still in stealth mode. We plonked them down by the wardrobe. They looked bad. Actually they looked like someone had chucked the display around the hotel and then rubbed himself all over with them. Which in essence was what I had put them through.

"If we get away with this one Marco, I will buy you a cigar." Ahmet said, without any sign of his usual broad grin.

Then, pointing towards the corner of the room. "Tell me Marco. What are those square things that look like suitcases? They are fucking suitcases! How did you not see them when you walked out of the room? You utter utter twat. Why did you think the guest had gone - all their stuff is still here!"

He was right, I just hadn't noticed them. The guest must have packed and gone downstairs to check out. She would now be waiting for her car whilst the Concierge sent someone upstairs to collect the bags and flowers.

We both looked at each other and had the same thought at the same time. Someone would be on their way upstairs to collect the content of the room.

A key clicked in the lock.

Shit. Here we were in a room we had no right to be in, with a bouquet that appeared to have been attacked by a swarm of killer bees. And the Concierge was about to open the door. Do we hide? I hissed at Ahmet. There would be no time, and a couple of half hidden mini-bar attendants would be a lot harder to explain that a couple of chumps in plain sight.

In wheeled the gold metal arched luggage rack from the Ground Floor Concierge Office. A smartly dressed man in a green suit and close-cropped ginger hair walked in behind it. "Oh hi Ahmet. You OK?" He said whilst loading up the cases and placing the flowers on top.

"Yeah I'm good. Have you met Marco, he's our new guy in Mini-Bars." Ahmet was as cool as a cucumber.

"No I haven't. But I think I saw you when you had your interview. I'm Steve from Concierge." He offered me his hand, before pushing his trolley with the cases and flowers on it through the doorway and closing the door behind him. His casual air made me think that finding mini-bars staff in a room, looking decidedly suspicious, was just a daily occurrence.

We looked at each other. "What just happened?" Ahmet asked me. I could only reply that nothing ever seems to go as you expect in this place and I was starting to wonder if I was living in some weird parallel universe. Ahmet, as it turned out, was a Dr Who fan and appreciated that suggestion.

I wouldn't see Steve again until the Christmas party a couple of months later. There I asked him if he thought it was strange that the last time we had met, he found Ahmet and I seemingly just standing around in one of the third floor rooms.

Steve replied enigmatically, "You see, when you've worked in hotels as long as I have, there is nothing that Ahmet does that would surprise you." Of course it made me wonder what else he had found Ahmet doing in the past.

Steve added an equally cryptic footnote. "You remember the day I met you in the hotel?" I felt an unease starting to embrace me. "Something strange happened when I got down to the foyer. The guest whose cases they were didn't recognise the flowers that I had brought down from his room."

His? Surely Steve meant her? And then it dawned on me. We had taken those blooms back to the wrong blooming suite. Whether the opera singer missed her bouquet, I shall never know.

Day 7

The last day of my first week and my second day off. After the panic of the flower incident I needed to calm down. I could see that there was no way that I was going to get home this side of Christmas to pick up more things, as the rota worked against me.

I'd noticed a lot of people on the tube listening to music through tinny headphones and thought that could be an answer to my lack of entertainment. The small 12-inch black and white TV that Ann had left in my room the day before could only get two of the four channels, so it was BBC2, the new Channel 4 or nothing. The choice was seriously serious programmes or a commercial channel that didn't have any ads to fill its commercial breaks, as nobody watched it.

I needed to hear some music. Not least as I had the Echo and the Bunnymen tape burning a hole in my coat pocket. So I went off to town and found the nearest Dixons next to Bond Street tube station.

Thanks to Barclaycard, I was soon the proud owner of a Sony Walkman 4. An all-silver box which had a Graphic Equaliser on the side, with small plastic knobs to slide to get the best tone. I didn't realise that feature made absolutely no difference because of the inferior headphones that came with it. Even so, the sound was like nothing I had heard before, and I was going to crank it up to 11 to drown out my tinnitus. It would have been so much better if I could hear the words the singers were singing.

The Bunnymen tape went into the slot and I was away. No more Rick Wakeman and Mike Oldfield for me. I had found my future. Heads will roll.

I looked at the Filofax in my coat pocket and the camera that I had slung over my shoulder and thought fleetingly, I wonder if they will ever build something that was like a Walkman with a camera and personal organiser on the side of it? Maybe even one of those massive brick phones too. Nah. It would weigh too much. You'd have to carry it around in a wheelbarrow. It would never catch on. Much better to keep all that stuff separate and just use what you need when you need it.

By now I was hungry and was just down the road from the hotel. I thought maybe I could just nip in to say hello to whoever was on shift and grab a sneaky lunch whilst I was there. So I did. Fortunately Security weren't in their box, so I didn't have to clock in. I did get a couple of odd looks as I was out of uniform, but I found Jean-Mick eating in the canteen with a couple of the porters so I joined him.

J-M was suitably impressed with the Walkman and a big conversation kicked off about whether my Walkman 4 was any better than the earlier models. It was certainly cheaper.

I finished lunch and decided that I would try to walk as far back along the tube line as possible before I got tired. It was something to do after all. Sightseeing and fitness all rolled into one.

A police cordon had been put up on one of the corners of Selfridges. Blue and white tape was rigged up between lamp posts to create an exclusion zone and various police officers in high helmets were ushering people away from the store.

This was prime shopping time on a Saturday and Oxford Street was very busy.

I crossed over and headed north up Duke Street, on the opposite side of the road from Selfridges, as the side nearest the shop was inaccessible and blocked off by the plod.

I wondered what was occurring. I stood there for a couple of minutes in the crowd then had a thought. If anything interesting did happen I had my camera with me, so I took off the lens cap and pointed it towards the shop. Echo and the Bunnymen continued to play at full volume in the headphones. I doubt that the people around me appreciated listening to the leaking sound, but I didn't care, my career as a photojournalist was about to start.

When I got a tap on the shoulder I assumed it was a disgruntled bystander who didn't want to hear the noise creeping out from the headphones. I continued to look through my camera and noticed that three or four police inside the shop were pointing out of it and looking agitated in the process. Are they pointing at me? I thought and this time the tap on my shoulder was more like a thump. Come on mate, there's no need for that!

I span round angrily ready to confront the rude person who had manhandled me, only to find it was a uniformed policeman. I struggled to turn off the Walkman and he had to repeat what he was saying, the third time he pushed the headphones off my ears.

"Who do you work for?" He asked. What? I was genuinely confused. I told him I worked for the Jupiter Hotel. "No numpty. What newspaper? Are you freelance, or do you work for a newspaper?" Now I was really baffled. I explained I was just a shopper, here is my Dixons bag with the packaging of the Walkman I've just bought. I work just over the road, here is my ID card.

"Why the camera then? Come over here, we need to do some checks." I was pushed towards a wall and by now there were more people looking at me than at Selfridges and the potential bomb display. The sideshow had become the main event.

Three more uniformed police surrounded me. I couldn't help but laugh. This was ridiculous. I was being pinned to a wall for no reason other than sightseeing. What about all the other tourists? I decided to be compliant, but wanted to make it clear I wasn't happy about what was happening. The policemen probably thought I was just a jerk.

I was searched and frisked. I don't know why. They just said they needed to do it and the dog handler who had pitched up looked like he was ready for some action if I didn't sit up and beg. I'd been chased by an Alsatian when doing my after school paper round and I had no plans to repeat the performance of boy versus dog for the tourists, many of whom were now taking *my* photo! They weren't the ones being arrested, however. This was the first time I had been body searched and as I had nothing untoward on me, I had nothing to worry about. But I felt guilty nevertheless. I was under suspicion, so I had to look suspicious.

Then came the analysis of the camera. "Some of our officers spotted you taking photos of the shop. Is this an actual camera?" I confirmed it actually was and impertinently asked what else did they think it could have been.

"The IRA have got some very sophisticated bombs nowadays. This could have been the trigger to set one off."

I pointed out to him that if a bomb had gone off he and I

would now both be dead, if not seriously injured, given that we only about 20 feet away from the shop front. He agreed with my logic and then said, "True, but maybe you are a suicide bomber."

They wanted my details. I had to provide evidence of who I was and where I lived etc. I questioned if I was obliged to give them. The look of pure hatred from the policeman who had first tapped me on the shoulder made me think that there wasn't a choice. Lucky for me I had put the copy of my contract at the Jupiter in my Filofax so showed them that.

"So you work at the hotel over the road right? And you live in Willesden Green right?" That's right officer.

"OK, well this time we are not going to take any action against you, but I must let you know that I am going to caution you not to do this again."

That's don't take photos of shops from a public right of way? You need to learn your law my friend, I thought but didn't dare say.

Time to catch the tube home, pot noodle, two Twix bars and two tins of Castlemaine, to accompany BBC2 Saturday night TV. I was starting to build a love of documentaries, especially as mainstream TV on Saturday nights tended to be punishment for people who didn't have a social life.

Crank up that electric fire until bedtime, but not beyond, and look forward to a day shift tomorrow.

Mental note: when dealing with the police in future, tell them to concentrate on catching real criminals.

Week 2

My Sunday shift started with a restocking of one of the massive trolleys from the store in the office. The phone rang and a sleepy Joe Makris called over, "Marco, is for you. Is your Dad."

Suffice to say I took the receiver off him with a mixture of mild panic and embarrassment.

"Hello Marco, is your Dad." It was Richard at the end of the phone. "Sorry to have tracked you down there matey, but I need to warn you about something I've done, that involves you." I asked him to explain whilst trying to adopt a disinterested neutral facial expression that would be in keeping with my Dad telling me about the dog dying, my parents getting divorced, or some other home calamity.

"Well, you know how I owe Buddle a fair amount of cash? I thought that maybe I should do the decent thing for once and give him some of the £300 he wants. Only I don't have it. Harriet wanted me to pay for some gig tickets, so I did. It left me with pretty much f'all, for a change."

"But fear not my son. I started a second job yesterday. I'm now a part-time financial adviser. Well, I'm not actually doing the advice part. What I do is go to Leicester Square and stop English-looking people and ask them if they have a pension.

If they say no, I try to get their details off them. Then the sales people will flog them something they don't really want or need."

"They pay me £3.50 an hour and I get 5% of any money that the suckers spend on their insurance policies or pensions. They gave me a target of signing up five people a day. If I don't hit the target, they don't let me come back. And yesterday I signed up five people. So kerr-ching, the Buddle fund is starting to fill up. Either that, or Harriet gets to go to more gigs."

And what, exactly, did this have to do with me?

"You are one of the five people." I didn't understand. I was nowhere near Leicester Square and I was sure I hadn't bumped into any old school friend, especially Richard. I definitely hadn't talked to anyone about insurance and the police weren't signing me up to their pension scheme when they stopped me at Selfridges, as far as I knew.

"As I said, I have to sign up five people a day. So as long as they get names and addresses, I keep my job. It's no big deal. You'll get a call from the office, so just tell them you changed your mind."

Thanks friend!

About five minutes later the phone rang again. Joe scowled as he passed it over.

"Hi this is Katie from Shureguard Financial. I understand that you met one of our reps, Richard, yesterday and expressed an interest in insurance and pensions products."

For some bizarre reason I couldn't bring myself to say, 'No, I think I've changed my mind.' Maybe I had been brought up with good manners, or I was just too passive – I had never answered a sales call before. She seemed like a genuinely nice person. She was just doing her job and who was I to deny her that? As it was I didn't have a pension, so what would be the harm in having a chat about options.

My weakness exploited, I somehow agreed to meet one of their reps at my bedsit the following evening to go through the best options for me. At this point, all I knew about pensions was that my Dad would rather put his money into one than take us on holiday and that his advice was to put the same percentage of your salary into a scheme as your age.

Aged 18 and with a surplus disposable income of exactly minus £50 a month, I could see straightaway that this would be a very awkward conversation. I didn't have 18 pence to invest, let alone 18%.

————

7 pm the next day and the doorbell at Dartmouth Road rang. I nipped out before Ann appeared – I was pretty sure that having people in the room after dark wasn't allowed. (It turned out it was OK, so long as she knew about it. Talk about a passion killer!).

The rep was a tall woman, probably in her late 30s, early 40s, who introduced herself as Caroline. I gestured to her to go into my room and I followed her in. She was dressed in a gray business suit, which included a jacket with oversized shoulders and some of the highest heels I had seen. I wondered how women could walk on those as I offered her a coffee and suggested she sat on the bed, given that I was suffering from a lack of furniture.

It all looked well dodgy and I was surprised she didn't run a mile. Perhaps the heels prevented that from happening.

"Do you rent this room?" she enquired. I could tell she was

127

really thinking, "What am I doing here?"

I confirmed my status as being a member of the bedsit community.

"So, Marcus, if I can call you that. As you know, I am from Shureguard and want to explain some different options to you that will secure your financial future."

Caroline then took the next hour to show me the contents of a folder with diagrams and pie charts, graphs and projections, throughout which I was thinking, this is so wrong on so many levels. I think I'm falling in lust with this older woman. My mind wasn't on investments. How long could I continue nodding and faking an interest? And how will I explain this to Alison in my next letter to her?

At the end of the presentation she asked me, "So what do you think? Can I put you down for a dual pension/life insurance option? We can do that for as little at £150 a month to start with and you will probably want to increase that as your salary goes up." What did she say? I was staring at the lipstick that had gone slightly over the edge of her top lip. My only offer in return was an embarrassed errrrr. Time to snap out of this – she wants two weeks' wages each month from me, for a scheme that I won't see any benefit from for about 50 years. No amount of daydream fantasy would be worth that investment.

I suggested that I needed time to think about it. That way I could let her down gently and hopefully she and I would at least get to talk one more time when I did. However, I suspected our relationship was over. Indeed, it was over before she even realised she was in it.

"Are you sure? I can't remember the last time a client asked if they could think about this. The figures are all here, you can either afford it, or not." She started to take a firm tone. Maybe the penny was starting to drop that she had made the trip out to Willesden Green for pretty much nothing, other than to give a spoddy 18-year-old a daytime fantasy.

"OK. Let me leave all this with you. Have a think and call the office when you've done enough exploration of the numbers. I'll call you if not." I told her I was already looking forward to that. I was. Was I? Was I just a silly little time-wasting boy in her eyes? How could I have been anything else?

She left me with a waft of her perfume that lingered in the room. Her scent was welcomed as I still hadn't found a way to wash my work shirts. They were lurking at the bottom of the wardrobe, festering, waiting to be put back on in desperation. I really was low-rent.

————

The following day, Ahmet picked up the office phone and told me that Shureguard were on the line. This time my mood was one of excitement mixed with terror. Perhaps Caroline was calling to ask me out.

A male voice came on the line. "Hi, this is Mike from Shureguard. I understand you met one of my team last night and she left you to think about our pensions/life insurance package." I replied that I was still thinking about it. This was now totally mad. I had no intention of starting a pension, nor getting life cover. I had abandoned the Caroline dream overnight and I was now just doing this as a favour to Richard. Get a grip! The dude is getting paid off the back of this totally awkward situation I'm in.

"OK. Well if you can let us have an answer as soon as possible we would appreciate that."

There then followed three days of calls to the office and an increasingly annoyed Ahmet telling me that Mike had called AGAIN and each time I just cringed. I didn't know how to say no. This was eating me up.

Every time I thought of the next call from Mike, a part of me died. I knew that it was over between me and Caroline before it had started – she must have gone back to the office and told her boss that she had been to see this really creepy young lad in Willesden who didn't seem to have a clue why she was there. Mike was getting more and more terse the more I told him I was still considering options.

I was on the 5th floor, one storey below the office, when Joe appeared from the fire escape exit. "Marco, that fucking Mike is on the phone again. I told him this is the last fucking time he should call the hotel. He begged me to find you. So get your arse up to the office and tell him to fuck right off. No more personal calls, you hear?"

I picked up the phone and apologised to Mike for keeping him waiting. I also told him that I now had the right amount of time to weigh up the options and to fully consider his kind offer, but it wasn't right for me after all.

"You could have said that to Caroline, asshole." Was his reply.

The following day I met up with Richard after our day shifts finished to go for a walk around Hyde Park, along Oxford Street, down Regent Street and across to Leicester Square. When we got there, I told him about the brush with his new employer and how I just couldn't bring myself to say no, how I had nearly made a fool of myself in front of an unattainable and entirely inappropriate woman and how my boss had banned me from taking personal calls in the office. Cheers mate!

"Ex-employer", he said. "Ex-employer. I only did two days.

I ran out of people I knew in London after day 1, Buddle and Judy weren't quite as nice about it as you were. On day 2 I had to resort to making up fictional members of the public, as after eight hours of standing there stopping strangers, I had a big fat empty clipboard. Unfortunately the office team are shit hot on following up leads and saw straight through it. One wrong number, OK. But five out of five? Nope. I may as well have told them I had met Mickey Mouse and he was interested in taking out insurance for Disneyland and a pension plan for Walt."

"Buddle is still chasing me for back rent, it's looking well shaky. Do you know anyone who wants to let out a room to a young hotel executive?" When he confirmed that he was indeed talking about himself, the answer was a resounding no!

We ordered two Pernods in The Brewmaster pub next to Leicester Square tube and spent another hour topping them up with water from the bar, until they were so dilute that we were drinking water with a hint of aniseed.

Once we had drained the last drop of taste, Richard suggested we decamped to the cheapest Chinese restaurant in Lisle Street, Soho. It resembled a cafe that had been hit by a bomb. None of the furniture nor cutlery matched and the walls were covered in a mixture of broken tiles and grease.

"This place isn't as bad as it looks." Richard assured me. "I have never been ill on their food. Mind you I've only been here once before and the person I was with didn't exactly get on with some of their interesting flavours. Lucky for me Harriet thought it was exotic and not a shit hole."

I had been to Chinese restaurants back home. They were considered a luxury and the place we always asked to go to when it was our turn for a 'birthday lunch'. The last one of those had been for my younger brother in September. The meal was largely unmemorable but for the fact that my Dad proclaimed, 'Bon Appétit!' when the waiter came to clear our plates at the end of the meal. It was his way of expressing his appreciation of the food, but he was berated by all five members of his family for at least a week afterwards. Numpty.

The Happy Cafe menu was a bit less easy to fathom. Granted there were the usual foo yungs and chop sueys, but I thought I'd go exotic, which was in keeping with the Pernod-induced mood I was in. Also, 'Duck's Web' appeared to be one of the cheapest options on the menu.

The waitress came over and we placed our orders. Duck's Web for me please!

"You no change", was her reply. I looked quizzically at her. "You no change. I bring food. You eat. You pay. You no change." I agreed I wouldn't try to change it. I suspected this was not a good idea after all.

Neither of us knew what Duck's Web was. I assumed it probably safe to think it had something to do with duck. This was eight years before I finally became a vegetarian and looking back, I think the brush with Duck's Web may well have started my travels down that pathway.

Our food arrived. Richard had gone for an equally cheap plate of noodles with bits of meat and veg in it. I discovered what I had ordered, and why I was being instructed not to change.

The 'web' part of Duck's Web turned out to be the skin that joins the toes of a duck's foot. So to our mild horror, I had been presented with a plate with eight feet on it, swimming in oyster sauce. Four ducks were waddling around somewhere on stumps.

It was a case of eat or go hungry. So I picked the skin off the feet in an attempt to find some meat. There was none. The dish *was* the skin.

As if this wasn't enough, Richard delivered another tale of woe.

"The hotel found out that I was moonlighting. I've been sacked from there too. Pretty impressive stuff hey? Lost two jobs in two days. So I'm not just looking for somewhere to live, but a job to go with it too. I'm not worried though, I've already had an interview with your sister hotel on Park Lane. Same job and more money than you get paid. I know that's mad isn't it? You would have thought they'd pay the same as it's part of the same group. Let's hope it happens."

I went back to Willesden Green, using the ticket I had bought that morning at Kilburn to get off the tube. I had an early shift the next day so would need some sleep, if not copious cups of coffee in the morning. I just knew that Richard losing his jobs would be a problem and not just for him.

Around midnight, there was a tap on my window. As mentioned, my room was on the ground floor next to the front door. I got out of bed and put a T-shirt on. Was this how burglars, rapists and murderers operated in London?

There was another tap and I could hear "Marcus, open the window", hissed from outside.

I turned on the light and pulled back the curtain. I could see the outline of Richard's mop of dark curly hair. He was nervously looking back across the tarmacked drive at the road as if hiding from someone.

I opened the window as instructed and asked him WTF? He climbed in pulling a rucksack and a guitar case over the windowsill.

"Hi Dude. Any chance I can stay here tonight?" What could I say? On the one hand I knew that it would be against Ann's rules, but on the other, it was past midnight and this was one of only two of my friends in London. There must be something desperate going on and a friend in need is... a pain in the arse when it came to this particular friend.

"I had a problem with Buddle when I got back to his. I think he had been on the wine or something. I was expecting him to tell me how much he loved having me in his house, but he went off on one about how lazy I was, how I took the piss, how I never put anything in the fridge, but was happy to empty it and of course, how I owed him nearly £400."

"Being on the dole now, there is no way I can get that money for him, even if I wanted to. I decided I had no choice but to flick him the vees, grab my gear and get out. I think that makes me currently officially homeless. But good news...." he said, plonking a bottle of wine down on my table, "I took one of his best bottles on my way out as payment for my company over the last few months."

Richard unrolled a sleeping bag he had tied onto his rucksack, laid it down between the bed and the window (well away from the room door, so that he wouldn't be immediately seen if Ann came in) and made a pillow out of his coat. "Any chance you could put the heating on?", he asked as he unzipped the polyester bag. I explained that was a negative, Captain Kirk.

I now seemed to have acquired a flat (broke) mate.

I had to get up shortly after going to sleep for my early shift. Richard was planning on moving onto my bed to continue sleeping. I told him to double-lock the door so Ann wouldn't come in and close the window after he left. Whatever he was going to do, he must not get caught. I knew that was like asking a pyromaniac to look after a lighter for me and hopefully the house would not burn down by the time I got home.

— — — —

When I did get back later that day, Richard was gone, but his gear was still there. I realised that he would be back later and would probably be sleeping on my floor again that night, unless by some miracle, he had found another place to live.

As predicted, my window was knocked about 8 pm and my old mate climbed through it. We spent the evening drinking Buddle's wine and speaking very very quietly to avoid any suspicion from other people in the house.

Richard took a coat hanger and fashioned it into a toast rack to hook on the front of the two-bar electric heater. The remains of a stale white sliced loaf were then warmed on the improvised toaster. It meant that we could have a most enjoyable, if very quiet, toast and wine party.

"Listen up. I've had a thought. I should be able to get dole money for accommodation. So how about I say that I'm living here. If you give me your rent book, I can send them a doctored copy in my name and I can get paid what you pay in rent. I can give half to you. So I will have a bit of extra cash and you won't have to pay so much to Ann."

I suggested that if we were to do that, which we weren't, then all that dole money should cover the rent. That way we would both live rent free, even though for Richard that would mean continuing to sleep on the floor, as there was no way I would agree to the concept of bed time-sharing that he had proposed as part of the deal. There was a line - and me sleeping on the floor of my own room was beyond it.

I also knew that defrauding the dole was basically a really, really, stupid idea and I knew it would only end one way if we tried it. I just needed to make sure I never left my rent book

135

alone with the resident arch criminal.

———

Having Richard staying in my room was a laugh and a night-mare in equal measure. I soon realised that he was infuriating and why Buddle had ultimately lost his rag with him. He was charming and maddening in equal measure. Maybe he had got through life changing the rules and manipulating people and situations too easily in the past. All he had to do was smile and people seemed to bend to his will. Perhaps I should try smiling more often.

For the next four nights there would be a knock on the window and his shadowy figure would climb in, carrying his guitar case. He had been busking on the tube stations in the West End and by all accounts (his account mainly) his renditions of The Boxer and All Along the Watchtower were making him a few quid, before the station staff moved him on. "Those Nazis don't appreciate free entertainment", Richard concluded.

Once through the window, there then followed the ritual toast-making session and he'd get into his sleeping bag pit by the side of my bed. To say that the mornings were greeted by a fug in the room was an understatement. During that time he didn't seem to remove his one pair of pants, nor venture into the bathroom. We were a couple of teenage dirt bags.

I'd put my uniform on and disappear off to work, whilst he climbed onto my bed. Every morning I would worry that one of the residents in another part of the house would spot him on the staircase going up to the toilet, or worse. We all needed to take a dump at some point after all.

On the fourth morning, as he left the house through the window, I told him that this couldn't be a long term solution. He would have to face the fact that he would need to find somewhere else to live and what's more that he would need to pay rent there too. He needed that job to come through.

"Chill. I only need maybe a couple more weeks. I think that my other brother is moving to London and he said I can crash there."

Two more weeks? I put my black trousers on and the least smelly shirt ready to leave for work too. As I was closing my door Ann, the landlady, appeared behind me.

"Hello Marcus. I'm needing a word. There is a man who lives over the road who tells me that he has seen a lad climbing through your window at nights. Would you mind telling me what is going on?"

I was rumbled. I felt my bollocks start to retract in fear. Honesty was probably the only policy, so I explained that it was my mate from home who had lost his job and his digs and was sleeping on my floor until his next place came free. It hadn't occurred to me that a more plausible excuse would have been to have said that he was my lover.

Ann wasn't impressed. She must have thought he was sharing my single bed. "Well now. You know that the rules mean I don't like guests in my rooms. And no overnight guests unless you agree it with me first – it's for fire regulations. If the house burnt down I need to know how many people are in it. What do you think the neighbours must think? There's a young man climbing through my window every night and leaving through it in the mornings. I'm minded to turf both of you out."

I felt like shit. I asked her if she could overlook it, so long as I promised to send Richard packing later that day. Ann said she would think about it. Fortunately she hadn't mentioned the home-made toaster, which really could have burnt the place down at any minute.

About 7 pm there was a knock on the window and Richard appeared. I pointed him to go to his right and I went round to open the front door.

"What's up? I thought the deal was to avoid the hallway as much as possible?" I told him that Ann had confronted me about my night-time visitor and he would have to pack up and find somewhere else to crash. Otherwise I would be looking for a new room too. The piss taking had to stop.

"OK. Understood. Any chance of a cup of tea first? I have some good news. I start at the hotel in Park Lane tomorrow. That mini-bar job came through. So things are on the up."

We went into my room and I put the kettle on. There was a knock at the door. Ann.

"Can I come in Marcus?" She didn't really give me a choice, the question was entirely rhetorical.

Addressing Richard directly, Ann wasn't going to pull any punches. "Now then, Marcus tells me that you are the lad who has been climbing through my window for the last few days. What's your name?"

"David", Richard replied.

"Well David. I can tell you that I am not happy about this. Not happy at all. It breaks my rules and I'm minded to ask Marcus to leave. But he's a very polite, well-behaved lad and until now has caused me no trouble."

'David' interjected. "I am so sorry for putting you and Marcus in such a difficult position. We're old friends from school and when the landlord at my old accommodation died suddenly, I thought of Marcus, as I don't know anyone else in London. I would have found a new place to rent straight away, but unfortunately, with my dear friend Mr Biddle now being deceased, and now resting in heaven, I wasn't able to get my deposit back. I told his sick daughter that she should keep it to buy food for her baby. All the other money I had, I gave as a donation to help his poor family organise an appropriate tribute to such a generous man. I then found myself without a job as the place I was working at had a massive fire after being struck by lightning."

She totally bought it. I was absolutely stunned. Talk about thinking on your feet. Richard had always been a bullshitter at school, but had this annoying charm about him that meant parents and teachers would always give him the benefit of the doubt and a whole lot more. It seemed that landladies would do the same. Having said that, my Mum's lasting memory of Richard is of him staying at our house one night after a school-time pub session and complaining about the pillows being too hard at breakfast the next day.

Ann replied. "Well Marcus and David. I have a proposal for you. There is a double room free upstairs. Why don't the two of you move up there? It will work out better for you as well Marcus as it is £200 a month, so £100 each. Come upstairs and I will show you."

Five minutes later we had relocated to what would have been the master bedroom at the front of the house, before the conversion into bedsits.

The room was L-shaped meaning that if we pushed the wardrobe slightly toward the middle of the room, we could place our beds at each end and not have to look at each other sleeping. Perfect. Richard now had his own bed and I hoped he had suitably hard pillows as well.

Ann said to Richard she would need a month's rent and month deposit, £200. But given the circumstances of his last rental, she would waive the deposit and he only needed to start paying rent from the following week, when my next payment was due.

The door closed, we argued over who would have the bed furthest away from it. I thought Richard had no case as he had nearly made me lose my accommodation after all. Amazingly he was willing to agree with me. I told him I was impressed by the way he had twisted Ann round most of his fingers and asked when was he going to tell her that his name wasn't David.

"I've got no reason for her to know who I really am, as long as I pay my rent in cash and avoid signing cheques. And as to the question about how I just charmed her into saving our arses, Jedi mind tricks, my friend, Jedi mind tricks."

I wondered if Ann would question why the post that was coming to the house for someone called Richard was being taken upstairs by David in Room 1.

Just a pity that he wasn't using those Star Wars powers of persuasion when he was stopping people in Leicester Square and flogging them pensions.

Week 3

Richard and I were getting into our domestic routine. I even bought some Daz washing powder as I realised that if I put my dirty shirts in the bath and ran a couple of inches of hot water over them, then stamped on them in the same way that a Frenchman would crush grapes, that mighty white power would help me to get most of the stench out. The dirty water told me it was a job well done as most of the London filth and body excretions flowed away down the plughole.

I would then hang the shirts up in front of the fire in our room. As part of the relocation, we now had an upgraded fire with four electric bars, set into the wall. It felt like luxury. After a couple of hours of dripping, my shirts were dry enough to wear. There would be a sizable damp patch on the carpet underneath, but that would dry out, eventually.

Creases were accepted as a problem, given that we had no iron. The received wisdom, received from Richard that is, was that they magically 'fell out' if hung up overnight on a coat-hanger by the window. He also had a technique of pressing shirts under his mattress, which never seemed to improve them. I just made sure that I never unbuttoned my burgundy uniform jacket as an extra precaution. If people couldn't see my shirt, they'd have no way of knowing I didn't own an iron.

Despite being a ficking fuckwit without a clue how to clean clothes properly, the mini-bars were going great. The team had got into a groove. The hotel only had guests on floors 1 to 4, so it was easy for the day shift to get the rooms covered off by mid afternoon, meaning that we could spend the rest of the day in the office with Joe or Ahmet, or both of them, doing what they did best. That involved smoking foreign cigarettes in Joe's case, looking at the ever-increasing pile of porn mags, listening to tall stories of life before wedded bliss from Ahmet and trying to work out if Didier was indeed gay.

———

It was during Week 3 that we had our first stock-take. I couldn't understand why Joe and Ahmet were so excited about the visit of an Irish guy called Brian, who arrived in a black suit, having escaped the Accounts team office which was based in the cellar.

"Welcome to the 6th Floor", Ahmet said. He presented Brian with a list of everything that was stored on our office shelves and a list of the amount of stock that the trolleys had on them.

Brian proceeded to start to tick off the list, counting cans of soft drinks and bottles of fizzy water, as well as the lines of miniature spirits, with the end of his rubber-tipped red pencil. It looked like Ahmet's list matched with what was there, given the number of ticks and lack of corrections being made.

Floor Service Mohammed appeared in the doorway.

"Hey Ahmet. Has Brian been yet?"

"Get lost Mo, he's here now", Ahmet hissed back.

Ahmet then picked up a cardboard box containing various empty bottles that had either been broken by us over the last couple of weeks, or found with the seals broken, meaning that they couldn't be sold as they had probably been opened by a guest who changed their minds when they realised it wasn't a free bar.

The box also had a few Cokes that had touched the cooling element in the fridge, which made the contents freeze, before buckling the sides of the cans. There were also a handful of miniatures that had arrived damaged when we had added them to our stock, usually where the seal on the bottle cap wasn't quite intact. The breakages box was basically all the crap we couldn't sell to the guests.

After Brian left, Joe explained to me and Jean-Mick, who had also finished his round early, how the audit worked and why Mohammed was at the door. It seemed like Joe had an accounting scam going that went back well into his days working in Floor Service.

"Accounts know how much stock we had taken from central stores in the cellar. They know how much we have sold, because they add up totals of the dockets we write that get charged to guests' bills. The difference is where? Is the stock held in the office and on the trolleys. So for example, if we had £500 worth of stock from the cellar, we sold £300 worth, then £200 would be left in the office or on the trolleys, right?" It all seemed to make sense.

Now here was the interesting part, and the part that Mohammed was involved in.

"Some of the stock in the office gets damaged - the breakage stuff in the box that Ahmet gave to Brian. So say that was £50 worth. The £200 stock in the office could then be divided into £150 of good stock, which we would use to fill up the fridges and £50 of shit bottles and broken stuff that are no good to sell. As long as our stock holding balances, no arse gets kicked."

I'd lost him.

Ahmet wrote on a piece of paper, '*Stock from stores = Stock sold + stock in office + stock on trolleys + broken stock*' and finished off the equation with a big tick as a flourish.

"If that balances Brian is happy."

So what did that have to do with Mohammed?

Joe explained. "Well Marco. Mohammed is an alcoholic and for him to work in Floor Service is not good. He is surrounded by booze, but manages to hold it together. When he started working here he was in the Grosvenor Bar downstairs as a waiter. Those were bad times for him."

"Mohammed and me go back a long way. Once a month he pays us a visit and we have a drink."

Ahmet took the box of breakages and replicated the contents with good stock from the store room shelves. So there were two lines of bottles on the office table. One all broken and the other brand new. Jean-Mick and I still looked confused, especially when Ahmet swept the broken bottles back into the cardboard box and put it back on the shelf.

"You see Marco and John, all that Brian cares about is his numbers. Each month he counts our breakages and tells us to put the contents in the bin now that they are accounted for. But we know better. We keep those bottles for next month and next month he counts them again. Because he is the numbers guy, he doesn't notice that he is counting the same stuff each time. Every time he counts a broken bottle, we can drink a good one. It all balances and Brian is happy."

"It gets better each time because that fucking idiot Andrew keeps breaking stuff and every time he does it, we just add the broken bottle to the box. Each time he drops a whiskey, it means Mohammed can have a whiskey after audit day. If we don't throw the broken bottle away, and Brian carries on counting it, Mo can have a whiskey every month."

"By this time next year, one broken bottle will be counted 12 times and we will have taken 12 bottles of good stock off the shelves for our party. Why do you think I don't seem to give a shit when you boys drop miniatures, or knock the labels off in the trolley? When I was in Floor Service, by the end of the year, we would have enough bottles that none of us ever had to buy booze for Christmas."

Mohammed reappeared, looking over his shoulder and cautiously into the office to check if Brian had gone. "Come in Mo. What do you fancy?"

The office door was closed and locked and the monthly audit party started. Half an hour later there was a knock on the door and Joe swiftly pushed the empty bottles into the bin. Outside was Andrew. He had arrived for his late shift.

"Come in Andrew", Joe slurred at him. "Mohammed is up here to have a cup of tea, aren't you Mohammed?"

Mohammed had already started to slip past Andrew towards the office door, pointing at the couple of Jim Beams he held up behind Andrew's head and mouthing 'Thank you'. One thing he had learned over the years in the hotel was to only drink booze with people who he trusted. He had a reputation among managers for being a drinker, but so far none of them had ever caught him with a bottle in his mouth.

"Eh OK." Was Andrew's reply. He knew something odd was going on, but he didn't know what. His dark brown eyes flicked between each of the secret drinking club members. We all tried to keep our poker faces going, but Jean-Mick couldn't hold it and started to laugh. Andrew had been there long enough to know that there was always something going on with Joe and Ahmet and he also knew that if he was to get promoted, it would be best not to know the details.

It was probably the reason why Joe and Ahmet were wary of him. They knew he had ambition, but lacked common sense and raw intelligence. He was quite likely to report one of their scams to Mr P, or even worse the Security desk, thinking he was in some way being helpful to the hotel. Thinking about it, dobbing in people who were ripping off their employer would usually be seen as a good thing to do. Joe made sure the rest of us would never do that to him as he made us his accomplices. You were either part of his gang of thieves, or confronted by a wall of silence (and the odd Gallic snort of laughter). Clever.

"I'm just going to go to central stores and get some more 7Ups", said Andrew to create his escape route.

After he had gone, and emboldened by the three miniature bottles of Cointreau I'd just had, I asked the others if they thought Andrew looked like a zoo animal.

"He's a fucking penguin!" Joe exclaimed and the office erupted into much hilarity, as the four of us waddled around it, shouting "Eh" at each other, whilst sipping from miniature bottles of booze and the litre bottle of whiskey I'd found on my morning shift a few days before.

My shift was coming to an end and my head was by now spinning. I bade the guys farewell. Joe stopped me.

"Hey Marco, before you go, I want you to look at something." He pulled a small suitcase out from under the desk.

Ahmet jumped in, "Marco. Don't forget what I told you about this." He tapped the side of his hooked nose with his index finger and walked out of the office.

"Look Marco and John. I want you to look in this suitcase with me." He unzipped the flap of the case and plonked it on the table. The three of us were now looking into it as if we had just opened a bag full of narcotics en route from Columbia. I was expecting to see lumps of dubious-looking natural products wrapped in clingfilm.

"I sell stuff to people like you two. It's all top quality."

"Is it stolen?" Jean-Mick asked.

"Hey, come on." Joe looked genuinely hurt. "I buy it from a man at the docks. He gets it from China. It has really good prices because we are not buying in the shops. Most of this stuff you can't get in the shops anyway." Joe started to rifle through his bag of delights.

"Marco. You should get a present for your girlfriend and John, you should get something to send to your Mummy in France. When is her birthday?"

"Not until June", J-M replied.

"OK. You buy it now and you won't have to worry about it later", was Joe's logical suggestion.

Jean-Mick offered Joe two upturned palms and exclaimed, "Purff. Is not for my mother Joe." He took a step back and sat down on the chair that Mohammed had been having his bender on an hour before. Somehow J-M had listened to Ahmet and been able to dismiss Joe's bag of shite before he was sucked into it. Whereas I, on the other hand, half-pissed and with an inability to say no to anyone, for fear of upsetting them....

"Now Marco. What do you want to buy? I've got these great watches and here is some perfumes. It's all good stuff. You won't know the names of it, because it comes from China, but all the shops over there sell it." I picked up one of the watches in a cellophane wrapper. It looked like a metal casing but felt too light. It was painted plastic. I told Joe that my girlfriend had a watch and she would only wear Chanel Number 5. If I

147

gave her anything else, she would dump mė.

"OK. What about this. I sell these for £15 but because is you, you can have it for £7. They cost more than £20 in the shops in China."

I took the black plastic item off him. It consisted of two oblong boxes about 6 inches long by 3 wide and 2 deep that were joined together along the fattest side by a coiled plastic cable. And this is what exactly?

Joe took the item off me and pulled the two halves of the box apart. "Is a radio see?" Jean-Mick started laughing and I studied the radio more closely.

The two halves were joined at the base by a flimsy connecting wire. One half was obviously a speaker, with a circular set of punched holes in it at the base. The other half must be the receiver as it had a dial in the middle, which served to tune it in. At the top of the speaker box I now saw a pair of stylised boobs had been added in white. Below those was a hole, into which the tuning knob from the radio part fitted. The phallus also served to hold the two halves together. The penny dropped. It was basically two black boxes having sex.

"Is funny no?" Joe suggested. "You should give this to your girlfriend and she will think it is sexy. The radio is fucking the speaker. See?"

I asked Joe if it even worked. "Of course it fucking works. You need batteries for it. I would show if I had any. So you take this for £10 to give to your girlfriend. How much more money you got? You can't buy this fucking radio in the shops. Get it? 'Fucking radio'? I'm too clever for you Marco."

"Didn't you just offer it to me for £7 Joe?" I asked him. Maybe I was too clever for him. I had spotted that one.

"Hey come on Marco. You calling me a cheat? I'm not a cheat

or a liar. I said I sell them for £15 and said I could let you have it for £12, but £10 is my final price. Is a fucking bargain."

I didn't want to upset the man further, so apologised.

"Let me show you these rings. Genuine 50 carat gold. See, it has '50' written on the back. How many you want? I can sell them to you for £20, or £25 for two. You can make them bigger to fit your finger by rubbing the inside down a bit with a file."

For some reason I found myself saying yes to the radio just to get him off my back. I justified the purchase on the basis of it being worth the laugh and only later realised that he had indeed put the price *up* whilst he was demonstrating it to me. When I embarrassingly showed it to Richard later and suggested that I gave it to my girlfriend at Christmas, his only comment was, "You think Alison is going to find *that* funny? Good luck with that one mate."

I did indeed post the radio to her a few days later, after establishing that it just about picked up AM stations if held at the right angle. I explained that it wasn't a love token, but a reminder of the nightmare that working with Joe could be at times. The gift was a joke in every respect. She didn't appreciate the sentiment. We were heading for a split and the radio was never spoken about again. I had a mental image of her showing it to her new Uni friends and all of them having a great laugh at my expense. Especially that Keir bloke. He'll be mocking me in his legalistic tone, looking all muscle and gelled hair in his Big Country outfit. No doubt he would be using it as more evidence as to why I deserved to be dumped and, given all the circumstances of the case, he would be offering her a shoulder and more to cry on. Bloody law students.

— — — —

The day after the audit booze session, which led to me buying that thing from the cunning Greek-Cypriot-Malteser, I had two brushes with Security. Or so I thought.

Firstly, on arrival for my late shift, the guy on the security desk by the clocking in machines stopped me and asked if he could check my bag. I must have had a dodgy air about me, left over from being part of Joe's breakage scam the day before.

I nervously passed over a carrier bag that had my Walkman, my Filofax and a couple of Twix wrappers in it (breakfast). I thought, this is a bit fucking strange. I'm going INTO work, not leaving it. If I was going to steal from the hotel, surely the check should be when I go home.

"Is this yours?" The guard asked, holding up the Walkman. I confirmed that is was.

"How does it compare to the earlier Walkmen? I'm thinking about getting one. Where did you get yours from?" I told him it was from the nearby Dixons and I chose that one because I could only afford £80. Some of the earlier models were well into the hundreds.

He seemed grateful for the information – indeed the following day when I came in, I could see him in his security box reading a tabloid with a set of headphones covering his ears. I thought if the PLO were round the corner waiting for Israeli flight crews to appear, this guy will be totally useless. But I had a mate in Security now, so hopefully I wouldn't get searched again. Not that I was dodgy - but every time I left the hotel I couldn't help but feel and look guilty.

The second part of the security story was most intriguing.

It was 3 pm. I was on the second floor, half way round my fridge checks. I knocked on room 232's door and announced "Mini-Bars" in the usual way. Inside a woman's voice called me to come in.

I asked if I could check her mini-bar. She said sure and lay down on her side on the bed and watched me go across the room to where the fridge was housed. It hadn't been opened.

I stood up from my crouching position, and turned round to thank her for letting me in. At that point I realised that she only had a bathrobe on, and it was barely covering her body.

"No worries." She replied in a Italian accent. "I will be here again tomorrow at this time, so you can come and check it for me again."

I explained that we worked a shift pattern, but there was a strong chance that I would be doing the second floor again.

I'd pretty much forgotten the encounter, until the following day I was slated to cover the second floor and dutifully started my rounds.

When I got to 232, I thought she wouldn't be there again. It had been a wind up on her part. She wanted to see me squirm and she definitely managed that. I must have blushed when I realised what she was, or wasn't wearing. Once nearly bitten, twice, thrice and four times, shy.

But she was in her room. Again she let me in. Again she lay on the bed and watched me go to an untouched bar. Again, she was naked but for the bathrobe, although this time even more flesh was on display, as well as pair of black stockings. I thanked her for letting me check her bar and started to walk out of the room, trying not to look at her.

She stopped me as I walked towards the door and said, "When do you finish? If you like you could come back here and we could open the fridge together?" I was flattered. Here was a beautiful woman who wanted to get to know me better. I told her 6 pm and I would see what I could do. By the time I left the room I was thinking, 'What the hell are you thinking! You should have said no. Now you're going to have to make a decision.'

The rest of my round was a bit of a blur. This sort of thing doesn't happen in real life. I'm 18 and from the country. I've only had one serious girlfriend before, who I lost my virginity to shortly before we finished our A levels. I have all the sex appeal of a damp B&B mattress in Blackpool and my uniform was particularly stinky that day. What exactly did this temptress in 232 see in me?

And then I clocked it. She must be one of those staff members that the hotel had put in place to try to corrupt us into bad behaviour. She was taking her role as mystery shopper very seriously!

I pushed my trolley along the 6th floor to the office. Ahmet was sat in there cutting his finger-nails onto the floor with the pair of scissors I had borrowed for my self-inflicted haircut. I explained to him what had happened earlier in room 232, and how it had also happened in the same room the day before.

"I take it you are going back?" was his only reply. Was he kidding me? I didn't want to get caught by an undercover, barely covered, security operative. It was obviously a honey trap designed to catch me. I didn't want to be the poor guy that fell into it. Although what a way to go...

"Let's look at the facts Marco. All of the Floor Service guys are gays, except for Mohammed and no one would want to go near him. She's probably been ordering sandwiches all day and waiting for a Floor Service waiter to come and give her a seeing to. By the time you got there she was desperate. No offence, but you know what I mean."

I started to think that Ahmet had been looking at too many of his porn mags. This sort of thing didn't happen in real life.

"All I can say is, be grateful that you are talking to me and not Joe. Joe would be down there by now filling more than her mini-bar." Ahmet started to chortle at the thought of this. The word chortle is not often used, but in this case he absolutely was.

"You've got to go back at 6 o'clock. If you don't I will start thinking you are batting for the other side with Andrew."

I reminded Ahmet of the security briefing.

"I can tell you that the staff that security put in the rooms don't get half undressed when they are trying to bribe you. They're more interested in seeing if you will take a monkey or a pony as a tip. They leave half bottles of whisky opened, marked on the side with a felt tip pen, to see if any of the maids help themselves when cleaning rooms. It's that sort of low rent, low hassle stuff. I doubt that any of the security people have ever worn black stockings at home, let alone at work. Can you imagine Igor by the clocking-in machines turning up for work in that gear?"

I made a weak joke that the stockings would make an interesting staff uniform even for Andrew.

"Setting up a sting like this isn't their style. And you know what Marco, you will be doing us all a favour, cos if it turns out she is waiting down there with your P45 because you took the bait, then all the rest of us will know not to do it ourselves. Of course, I'm not interested anyhow, being married with a daughter and all that. But when I was younger, I would have."

You still are so so young, I thought.

So Ahmet's advice was basically for me to go back to her room to see if she was indeed just genuinely interested in me, and if not I would get fired. That's me, with an ill-fitting jacket, dirty shoes and an off-white shirt full of creases. Not to mention the self-inflicted haircut. Me, who had only had one serious girlfriend and would probably wet himself if touched by the hands of an Italian angel. Anyway, why was I even thinking about the possibility? I loved my girlfriend and there was no way in a million years I would betray her with the gorgeous, sexy, stocking-clad, curvy and sensual guest in room 232.....

On balance, there was no contest, I would have to stand her up. Security had beaten me.

— — — —

I was in the office a couple of days later with Joe. He stood alongside me, lent into me and put his hand on my shoulder, like a dad would do when he was about to tell his son a secret. He spoke in a quiet intensely sincerely voice, his sad eyes piercing mine.

"Now Marco. Ahmet told me about 232. Did you fuck her?" I confirmed that I had gone straight home from work and whilst the offer of a drink was appealing, it wasn't worth losing my job over.

"You are a fucking idiot Marco. No way was she Security. They wear tan stockings, not black, the same as the ones Housekeeping wear. None of the Security team from the other hotels are Italians either. If you had said she was Spanish, or Bulgarian, then maybe I would have been a bit worried that it was a stitch up. Although maybe not the Bulgarian, who looks like she does shot putt. They send her in to sort out the really difficult cases."

I confirmed that the woman was, as far as I could tell, not Bulgarian, but I could have mistaken the accent as Italian. Maybe she was indeed a Spanish honey trap.

"You missed your chance to be made into a man Marco. If you want I can ask Mr P to transfer you to Floor Service and let his bum boys have a go on you."

I told Joe that wouldn't be necessary.

"OK Marco. I get it. You love your girlfriend and you are just a little boy with a little cock, who doesn't know what to do with it. The next time you get an offer like 232, you tell me and I will sort the problem out for you."

Sometimes, no most of the time, in this job it was difficult to know if what I saw, or was told, was real or a massive wind-up. Would Joe really go to pay guests a visit like the one I had failed to do? Was he just having a joke at my expense? He did seem genuinely disappointed with me. I knew that Ahmet had a theory about him and the Housekeepers, but I hadn't seen any real evidence, other than him flirting with them along the corridor. He seemed to know the make up of the sister hotels' security teams' female members a little too well. Unless of course that was bluff, Joe style.

I had decided to stay in London for the experience, but was getting one hell of an education. Nothing like this would have happened had I gone off to do my Biology degree as planned. I was living in hardship, but living the life. I wondered what my mates back in the country would think if they knew. How many of them would have returned to room 232? Exactly zero. We all had little cocks.

— — — —

Later on during that shift I encountered a different naked woman on the 4th floor . The floor had only a few rooms occupied. I was at one end of the corridor and came out of a room, having finished restocking the fridge, when I saw her maybe eight or ten doors down.

She was sprawled on the floor, on her side, her long black hair down to her waist covering most of her top half.

My initial thought was I was imagining her. Then, given that we were the only two people there, I walked briskly down the corridor to see if she was real and OK. As I did, Mohammed came from the lift lobby at the other end and we arrived at the woman at the same time. We both knelt down over her and it was obvious she was semi-conscious. She was murmuring and had her eyes tightly shut.

Mohammed looked concerned. He said to me, "Get a pillow and a blanket", pointing at the room door next to us. He was cradling her head in his elbow. I unlocked the nearest room and grabbed some bedding from it. We covered her, taking care not to move her. Mo then instructed me to get help.

For some reason, rather than do the obvious thing and go into the nearby room to call Reception for help, I ran up the fire escape two steps at a time and breathlessly announced to Joe that there was a naked woman who had collapsed outside 415. She was in a bad way and that Mohammed was looking after her.

"Good joke Marco." He replied. After all, our previous conversation had been about the honey trap and I could tell that he liked my embellishment of adding Mohammed to the story. But his smile dropped when it dawned on him that this wasn't me trying to get him back for his comments about the size of my penis.

"Call Reception and ask them to get an ambulance. You wait here. I'm going to go down to help Mohammed."

I dialled 0 and quickly told them what was happening. And

as Joe instructed, I continued to wait. Joe appeared about 20 minutes later.

"Well done Marco. She's OK. The ambulance came and they took her to hospital. The paramedics said it was drugs and they think she will be alright. Security will probably want to talk to you about it. They are with Mo now."

Soon after the guy with the Walkman appeared and ushered me into the guest room opposite. Room 624, the one that Joe allegedly used as his love nest. There wasn't any evidence of recent debauchery.

I told him the story and he made a few notes. Basically a guest had taken an overdose, freaked out, taken off her clothes and fell into the corridor. Just another day in paradise.

I was quite shaken by this turn of events and Joe offered to finish my floor, which was only the three rooms. But it felt like an olive branch after the conversation about the Italian guest/security officer and I appreciated the bit of kindness in an environment that seemed to revolve around insults and put downs. I was living through crazy times and could see how anyone who had worked there for more than a year could be turned slightly psychopathic by it.

Perhaps there was a future in hotel work after all and Uni would just have to wait. Or was that crazy talk?

The next day was my day off, which I was glad about as the incident with the drugged woman had shaken me up.

———

I got up fairly early and headed into town. Walking from Bond Street to Leicester Square, down through Soho, I came across a bloke sat on a fold-up stool with a crowd around him.

"Come on ladies. Get your designer perfume here. Five different bottles for £25. It would cost you more than 100 quid in the shops."

"Ooo yes love, I'll have two sets", a woman in a fake fur coat said, flamboyantly passing him five crisp tenners. The seller made great show of putting the ten bottles into a plastic bag and the woman squealed in delight as it was handed over.

"Come along ladies whose next? Get them quick before they're gone. I took some of this stuff home to my wife the other day and she loved it. Even made my dinner instead of giving it to the dog." People started to wander off.

I could see that one of the selection of bottles in the box under his stool was Chanel No 5, Alison's favourite. I could buy the plastic bag of five bottles, give her the Chanel and maybe use the rest as Mum's Christmas present. I nipped over the road to the bank and took out £25. When I got back there, he was selling another bag to the same woman in the fur. Strange. She must just love this stuff. I handed over my money and walked away with a Co-op bag containing five 'designer' perfumes. I looked back over my shoulder and could see the street seller deep in conversation with a uniformed policeman. I felt very smug, I'd got it whilst it was hot.

Of course I wouldn't feel quite as smug when Ahmet told me that it was all a scam. "You shouldn't be smug, cos you're a mug Marco. It's flavoured water in rip off bottles and packaging. Even worse, it could have chemicals in it, like acid. The boxes are made by kids with Letrasets in the East End. I bet you any money that I could find at least 10 spelling mistakes on them. Was it Chanel you got or Channel?" He obviously thought that was a very clever comment.

"That bird in the fur coat. She would have been working with him. She buys the gear so that other people think it's kosher and want some too. When they move off, she will give the bottles back and he returns the money so that they can do their act somewhere else. It gets the attention of suckers like you. Bet you thought, 'She's keen, it must be good stuff'."

I told him he was wrong, even though I had thought that about the possible stooge. I was no sucker and he was just jealous that I had sniffed out a bargain. By the time I got home to my parents, Alison and I would have temporarily split, so she never did get to smell the street Chanel No5. I gave the contents of the plastic bag to my mum as her Christmas present.

A few days into the New Year she asked me whether I had kept the receipt. The perfumes all smelt the same and she didn't recognise the pong. Definitely not Chanel she said. I would look at my face in the mirror to see if I had GUM written across my forehead.

— — — —

After the encounter with the perfume seller of Old London Town, I found myself in Leicester Square. Which, along with the Crystal Rooms video arcade, was home to a lot of fast food and cinemas. There was an English Language school in one of the buildings and, unsurprisingly, the pavements were covered with Italian and French students, all dark hair and puffa jackets, bought to fight off the English cold. Every one of them seemed so happy as they ate their ice creams from the shop underneath their school building.

I had a whole afternoon ahead of me, with nothing to do. At that time I hadn't realised there was a wealth of museums and art galleries that I could have visited to warm up. I had come from a cultural void and had no bohemian frame of reference. I wasn't sufficiently aware of the artistic riches that London had to offer. The pinnacle of my cultural experience was watching buskers in Leicester Square and around Covent Garden market, five minutes away. In all the time I was in London, I didn't even see the Thames.

So I bought a ticket to see a film at the Empire Cinema, having been drawn in by all of the glitz and glamour that surrounded the huge logo on the side of the building. I was going to see 'Tron'.

Tron was basically a love story set in a computer game. It had been hailed as a masterpiece of computer generated visual effects. Up to then I had only ever played games on a Sinclair ZX Spectrum, so my expectations for the film were low. The plot line was indeed thin, although the effects were pretty amazing. Actors were racing around on light-cycles, trying to smash each other into walls.

There was something missing. I had never been to see a film on my own before. Early days would be with Mum or Dad and a combination of brothers, to see such epics as 'Waterloo' and 'The Aristocats'. The last two years had been with Alison, watching films on a screen half the size of the Empire's.

Like most teenagers, we created our own scenes with some pretty heavy snogging. In fact if you asked me what we went to see when we were going out at school, I probably couldn't give you one film title apart from 'The Equaliser'. It was early in our relationship and we were just 17. The film was an X (18 plus), so we were nervous about getting in. The lad in front of us in the queue was asked how old he was. He said 18. He was then asked what year he was born in. He gave it. The woman on the box office then shouted, "That'll make you 20. Get out!!." However, somehow we got in and were probably too nervous about being discovered to do anything other than watch Edward Woodward doing his hard man act.

I left Tron feeling depressed. The film was OK, even though the ticket was twice the price of those in Gloucester or Cheltenham. There was only one thing for it. I pledged to myself that I would never go to see a film on my own again.

I got home to find the avocado green porcelain wash basin in the bathroom smashed into a hundred pieces. The taps hung in mid air. After the day I'd had, I just couldn't absorb what I was looking at. I went across the landing into our room, where Richard was propped up on his bed reading a Time Out magazine. I asked him if he had been in the bathroom.

"Not since I came in. What's the matter, are you monitoring the number of pisses I take now?" I told him to follow me.

We went into the dingy bathroom and lo and behold the wash basin was still in bits. I hadn't imagined it. Hadn't he heard anything?

"I've only been in for about 20 minutes. It must have happened before that. There's no way this could have been done without me hearing it. It looks like someone has taken a sledgehammer to it." No shit Sherlock.

For a moment I wondered if he was telling the truth. But even in the warped reality that Richard sometimes inhabited, destroying bathroom fixtures and fittings wasn't a part of his repertoire. Not when sober and during the day anyway.

What to do? I guessed we should knock on Ann's door and tell her that it would appear that she had a psycho sink smasher living somewhere in the house. Richard stopped me.

"Think about it. We are probably the only two people in the house at the moment. She thinks I'm untrustworthy anyway, as I haven't quite paid the first load of rent yet. Also, what would the person do, who had done this? They would go and report it, that's what. That way any suspicions would be taken off them. It's a classic tactic that people who murder their families use. They go on TV to appeal for information when all the time they know who is guilty. She will look at us and think, they are too keen to let me know this has happened, they must have done it."

I thought this is mad. I am tired. I don't really give a fuck. Sort it out, don't sort it out. Tell Ann, don't tell Ann. I just want to go to sleep.

The next morning whilst the two of us were getting dressed, there was a knock on the door, and there stood Ann in what I believe is called a housecoat.

"Boys. Do either of you know anything about the bathroom?" she asked. We both shrugged. What about it?

"Come and see." We both walked across the landing in our shirts, pants and socks to take a look. Two lads without trousers studying the remains of a Victorian wash basin, trying to look shocked and surprised. Of course, we both looked totally suspicious instead. She must have known that we had been in there at some point in the evening, unless of course the exploding basin had happened overnight, in which case it would have woken the whole house and most of the neighbours as well.

"I just don't understand it. How did this happen? Who would do such and evil thing?" We both agreed, but explained that we were on the way to work so would appreciate the chance to put some trousers on. "Let us know if you find out anything, Ann", Richard added as a footnote as we returned to our room.

It was a mystery alright and one that remained unsolved.

Richard suspected the mysterious Mr Ann who had never been seen, but probably had a terrible temper and a massive hammer. This was probably part of a dirty campaign and he would be taking a crowbar to the toilet plumbing next.

Mr Ann had indeed only done half the job. The bath was intact and the toilet in the tiny room next door was untouched too (unfortunately by cleaning products as well). By the time I got back from my shift a new white hard plastic washbasin stood where the broken antique had been. 'That's progress for you', I thought as I put another slice on Richard's toasting rack and opened the copy of Men Only that Ahmet had handed me on my way out. I'd seen too much flesh already that week.

Week 4

H ilarity and horror was evident when I got on to the 2nd floor with my trolley, ready to check a fully occupied set of rooms.

As previously mentioned, the service lifts we used were a little unreliable. Not only did the cable stretch when our overweight trolleys were wheeled into them, but the doors had a habit of sticking too. And those lifts were slow. Miss one and you could be stood there for a quarter of an hour waiting for it to come back.

We all adopted a method of keeping the doors open, which was basically to let them close on you. They had a long rubber pressure pad on the edge, which flicked the door open when pushed. If the doors shut when you were trying to lift the trolleys out over the lip of the lift, the pads would bang into the trolley sides and make the doors bounce open again. This was also handy for people racing to get into a departing lift. Just stick your foot or hand out and let the pressure pad reopen the door for you. No button required.

But it wasn't quite so handy for Mohammed that morning.

I lugged my trolley out of the lift and started to push it towards the first room on my list. Mohammed was coming the other way, having delivered some food to a room down the other end of the corridor. We nodded our good mornings. "Busy?", "Yes, busy."

Suddenly behind me, I heard a crash and a cry for help.

Looking round, I saw Mohammed lying on the floor by the lift with the contents of his tray strewn across the carpet. His arm was straight up as if he was trying to attract the teacher's attention and I could see that his fingers were trapped between the lift doors.

"Help me Marco, I'm stuck!" He had tried to catch the lift after I left it, but he missed the pressure pads as the doors closed. His hand was now caught between them and the lift had moved off without him. Man and machine were now joined together.

Here we were again, me and Mohammed and a situation requiring some help, unless I could force open the doors and free him. They wouldn't move, but I heard an alarm bell buzz when I started to yank them.

I pushed the lift call button thinking the lift would come, the doors would open and he would be released. Some safety device had kicked in stopping the lift from moving as these doors were slightly ajar. Well, ajar by the width of Mohammed's squashed fingers.

By now Mohammed was going pale and started to pray quietly to himself. I told him there was no need for that. No one is going to die today. It felt like a line from Tron. I said I would go and get help, he just had to stay there. He had no choice anyway.

"No. Get Joe. Joe will know what to do."

It seemed a strange request. Maybe Joe had been a lift engineer in a previous life. But Mohammed was insistent so I ducked into the empty suite next to the lift lobby and called the Mini-Bar office number from the bedside phone. I told Joe where I was and what had happened.

Almost by the time I left the room and got back to Mohammed, who was still attached to the doors, Joe and Ahmet were there.

"Joe. Joe. I'm glad you are here. I need whiskey Joe. Whiskey. My fingers, they are gone Joe. Whiskey will kill the pain. Get me whiskey."

Joe turned towards me. "You heard him. Get him whiskey." I started to unlock the shutter on my trolley door.

"No, not that shit stuff we sell. We need a big bottle for this. Go back to the office and bring that bottle of Jack Daniels down." I didn't know what he was talking about. Ahmet explained that Jean-Mick had found it in one of the rooms and they were saving it for the next Monthly Audit Drinks.

Given that the lift was now out of order thanks to a certain Algerian's hand being fused to it, I ran up the nearest fire escape to the 6th floor. At the top, Didier was stood by the lift doors with his trolley. "Hey Marcoose. The lift she is broken."

I didn't have time to explain but told him to come with me. We rifled through the usual hiding places in the office and found the Jack Daniels wedged in under the table and behind a broken mini-bar that was due to go back for repair. Bingo.

Didier and I ran back down the same fire escape to where we expected to find Mohammed.

He was gone.

However a nearby Suite door was slightly cracked open and we could hear moaning and groaning punctuated with a very unhappy North African shouting, "Joe, where's my whiskey? I need whiskey! You promised me Joe, you promised me!!!"

I started to push the door open and Ahmet appeared on the

other side. Over his shoulder I could see Joe and Karl from Floor Service pinning Mohammed down to the bed by his shoulders. Ahmet was uncharacteristically abrupt, "You got it? Good. Piss off the pair of you and I'll fill you in back at the office later."

The lift was now working, given that Mohammed was no longer a part of it, so Didier and I jumped in back up to the 6th. Of course, when the doors opened we had to squeeze past his trolley that was still blocking the exit.

We went back to the office and Ahmet appeared about ten minutes later. He filled us in.

"After you left Joe and me there with Mo stuck in the door, he passed out. Joe picked up one of the knives from the tray Mo had dropped and was going to use it to push the sensor in the door to open it. Mo woke up, and thought Joe was about to cut his fingers off to free him. So he freaked out."

"We had to sedate him with a bit of a slap. In turned out that Joe hitting Mo loosened his hand. There was only one finger that was actually trapped – the rest were just in the crack of the door. So his hand was free. But we then had a knocked out Floor Service waiter to deal with. Joe had hit him pretty hard. I think his face will hurt more than his hand when he wakes up tomorrow. But it had to be done. No question."

"Karl came out of the lift. He had been stuck in it when the safety tripped it a floor up. He helped us move Mo into 201. What you saw was Mohammed waking up. He was a bit mental. I think he was in shock or something. But the JD calmed him down."

I told Ahmet that I was checking the 2nd and that my trolley was still down there. Should I carry on? He agreed.

Back on the 2nd floor, I could hear calmer voices coming from 201. I knocked on the door and asked Karl if everything was alright.

"He's fine. He's just a massive baby. Mohammed will always find an excuse to get pissed", Karl replied in his slightly nasal voice. In the room Joe sat on a chair next to the bed, where Mo was still lying and swigging from the bottle. He had a look of mild anger on his face - one side of which already had a bruise coming out. I could see that Joe didn't want to be nursing anyone from Floor Service and his prized bottle was being drained. If looks could kill Joe would have finished off the job.

Mohammed sat up on the bed clutching his wounded finger, although the trapped hand was still strong enough to hold the bottle. Less than half of the bottle of whiskey remained and Joe pulled it away from him. "Joe, Joe. Is hurting so bad. Give me more drink." Joe told him if he had any more he would have to give him more slaps to wake him up again later on. It was obvious that Mohammed held Joe in high regard, he was after all his senior in every hotel way. So Mo quietly stood up and walked past me, his bottom lip trembling as if he was about to burst into tears.

I asked Joe and Karl if we had to report this in the Accident Book that my induction pack had mentioned. Joe looked up at me with a thousand yard stare.

"Marco. When there is an accident we put it in the book. This wasn't an accident, Mohammed just wanted a drink. I've had to rescue him after getting caught in the dishwasher, falling down a fire escape, dropping a crate of glasses on his foot, getting run over by a maid's trolley in the middle of an empty conference room (which was a really weird one) and lots of other times. Every time his medicine is the same...whiskey. Why do you think the first thing he asked you to do was call me? He saw you and thought, 'Oh there's a lift door closing. Marco will be stupid enough to think my hand is stuck in it'. Or something like that. He does it to new people all the time when he's feeling thirsty."

Karl gave me a knowing smile. "I don't know why he doesn't just go out in the loading bay with the porters. They're on the bottle pretty much all the time. It would make our lives a whole lot easier."

The next day I bumped into Mohammed in the canteen. His finger was wrapped in a comedy bandage that made him look like he was wearing a snowball on his finger. His arm in a make-shift homemade sling. His right eye was half shut, but seemed perfectly OK when I enquired after his health.

"Is still hurting bad Marco. I can't carry a tray and Mr P has put me on light duties until it gets better. That could be weeks, maybe months. I think maybe it is broken and they have to chop it off."

Making sympathetic noises, I carried his dinner tray back to the hatch. It looked as if he had been able to use his poorly hand well enough to eat the free lunch provided to us.

I reported the Mohammed's medical verdict back to Joe. His reply consisted of just two words.

"Total. Bollocks."

Week 5

Sharing a room with Richard was turning out to be not as much of a nightmare as I had anticipated. He had even paid Ann his outstanding rent and looked good for the next month too.

We had fallen into a routine. Working three different shift patterns meant that one of us was often out when the other was in. One of us would usually still be up writing letters home or to our absent girlfriends, or trying to find nipples on Channel 4, when the other arrived home from a late shift. My letters to home usually included a line about my poor cash-flow and a cheque would arrive by return. If one of us was on an early, the other just about managed to stay asleep despite the noise. Because the room was so cold, we could get up and out of the house in about 10 minutes on a good day.

I was still a bit concerned that Richard only seemed to own one pair of pants, but maybe he just had a supply of very similar ones and I was worrying unduly. They didn't smell too bad, although I made a point of not getting close enough for a full inspection. We took great efforts not to appear gay to the other.

It was at this time that we realised our wages only covered rent and travel and the odd kebab, and if we were feeling flush, we would go to the Crystal Rooms on Leicester Square next to the Hippodrome and spend a quid in a video games machine. We got pretty good at flying our futuristic plane across a wasteland, avoiding cliffs and lumps of rock. It was money we really could have spent on something more useful. My spontaneous trip to see Tron the week before had wiped out most of my available spare cash, and I was relying on the dribble of tip money to pay for any luxuries.

Our entertainment became walking the streets of London. That came free. Richard had a trick he liked to play on tourists involving a lamppost. He would stroll alongside me, looking at me and talking shite in a very earnest way, and then walk into the first post we came to. Only he didn't. He would actually just kick the base of it.

Of course, a loud clunk and a lad clutching his face in agony would draw a lot of attention from anyone nearby, ideally girls in their late teens/early twenties.

I would play a supporting role by asking if he was OK and did he need an ambulance. He would stagger off as if dazed and confused and I would look to see if any passer-by would offer to help. No one ever did, although a few times people would politely say, "Are you alright?".

We used it as an attempt to get a bit of sympathy, but nothing else, definitely not any phone numbers. Looking back on it, it was probably the worst chat-up line in history and we both had girlfriends anyway. Richard hadn't briefed me on how we would convert a "Are you OK?" into "Would you like to go for a drink?" so the whole game was just a bit daft.

Our favourite walk seemed to be Leicester Square to Oxford Street via Soho. We'd cut across Chinatown over Haymarket, look at what was on at the theatres and then take a lot of sideways glances into shop windows in the centre of Soho, which was home to the kind of stores that would never appear in rural high streets back home. I saw some things there that I couldn't understand. I had no frame of reference. Why would anyone want to buy a rubber hand in the shape of a fist?

I didn't dare venture into any of the shops, which all had coloured plastic streamers obscuring the doorways, so it was hard to see in. Most of them also had either a balding old man, or an over made-up middle aged woman guarding the doors. I made sure I didn't catch their eyes as I walked past. 80's Soho was seedy, but that also made it a magnet to a pair of 18-year-old lads who needed their eyes opened.

We'd end up in the leafy Soho Square and from there stroll into the tourist town of Oxford Street and down to HMV. My tape collection was starting to grow nicely. I'd discovered Teardrop Explodes, Simple Minds and Siouxsie and the Banshees, as well as Joy Division and New Order. Those tips were being invested wisely.

— — — —

One day we were walking past the Raymond Revue Bar and Richard disappeared. Where had he gone? I retraced my steps only to notice him stood just inside the doorway of the dark blue painted, neon signed foyer. He was deep in conversation with someone I couldn't see.

Now I knew that Richard fancied himself as a ladies' man and having walked past the Revue Bar with him a few times before, I knew what the ladies in there would be doing on stage. They also appeared in some of the ads in Ahmet's magazine collection and he had told me I should, "Go and check it out some time when you've grown a pair." Ahmet the purveyor of the female form usually had a point, but I suspected this was Ahmet the perve talking.

I'd often wondered what it looked like inside, in the same way I'd tried to imagine the interior of Soho's sex shops, but would have never had the nerve to go in. I was just a frightened little country boy after all.

I took a step closer and could see a man in a black mohair sweater and a Beatles style haircut, maybe in his mid-20s, talking to Richard. I thought I vaguely recognised him.

"Marcus come in. Do you remember Ed? He worked in the music shop back home. He used to let me play the guitars after school. You must have come with me a couple of times." I realised that it was indeed Ed the Music Man. Richard and I used to go into his shop after school to mess about on guitars. I'd strum E, G, A and Richard would do his best Hendrix impersonation, but not before Ed had told us to keep the amps turned down and to take our belts off to save the guitars getting scratched.

"He's moved down to London and is working here. I noticed him as we walked past."

Ed explained that he had relocated in the summer and the bloke he was sharing a flat with found him the job here. His days seemed to consist of making sure the stages and backstage areas were tidy. He was basically a glorified cleaner, surrounded by bare boobs.

"Does that mean you spend all day with the girls?" Richard asked him.

"Yeah I do, but they're not all that. You've probably walked past a few on your way here. You wouldn't notice them until they get into make-up and put on a show. It's kind of weird, as most men would think this is a dream job. But once you get over the idea that you're surrounded by tits, it just becomes normal. The girls are just your everyday girls in the street who take their clothes off to pay the bills. It's not a sexual thing at all."

"Do you have any jobs going on stage?" Richard asked in all seriousness. I wondered if he was seriously thinking of becoming a performer. I could tell that he might have been, but he didn't have the capacity to think of this place as 'normal' like Ed did. He wanted to get paid for having a waking wet-dream. I'd seen him in his pants too, it wasn't something anyone in their right mind would pay money for.

Ed replied, "If you are talking about performing, forget it. It's all about the girls. I could ask the manager though. They do take on people every now and then backstage or in the box office and bars. The work tends to be casual, and the hours aren't regular. Only a few staff like me get a survivable income from it."

"The management prefer girls as waitresses and bar staff. In fact, thinking about it, they are all girls. So being a bloke, you're more likely to end up backstage or on security. But to be honest with you Richard, you're not exactly built like a brick shit house are you? I'd say you couldn't stop a fight in a girls' primary school playground, let alone break up a full-on brawl between a bunch of pissed-up perverts. And before you ask, we get at least one of those most nights. That's stag nights for you."

Throughout the whole of this conversation I was mute. I was partly overwhelmed by the publicity posters in the lobby, partly unsure of whether I would be confronted by a woman dressed in feathers, or a man in a dirty mac, and partly taken aback that only a few weeks ago the biggest thrill I'd ever had was watching Hot Gossip and Cleo Rocos on Kenny Everett's TV Show, when Mum and Dad weren't about.

Ed disappeared to find the manager and I begged Richard to leave. What was he thinking? This place wasn't for the likes of us. Even the music being played was like nothing I had heard before - dirty twangy guitars. Good old Link Wray, the soundtrack to many a striptease.

Richard didn't move. In his mind he was already behind the scenes in the changing rooms of showgirl heaven. He told me to calm down and he'd get me a job here too once he'd got his feet under the table, or on the stage, or wherever else he could find to put them.

Ed reappeared. "Sorry mate, we're fully staffed. Also the boss said he likes to take people on who are over 21. Aren't you two still at school? Maybe come back in a few years."

Crestfallen, Richard followed me out of the Revue Bar. Part of me was sad for him, but I was mainly massively relieved. I just wasn't ready for the stories he would have brought home from work and I suspect at some point he would have wanted me to go out for drinks with the girls. I just wasn't equipped for any of that. Call it shyness, naivety, or just being a yokel, but I still hadn't adapted fully to a sleazy Big City life. Joe and Ahmet were right, I was just a little boy with a little cock.

We headed back home via the HMV again where I picked up Tears For Fears' 'The Hurting' on cassette and another one of the early Simple Minds albums from their sale. I realised that I was starting to build a collection of the music that I had previously turned my nose up at when I was at sixth form parties. At least I hadn't gone down the route of Billy Joel, Springsteen, Supertramp and the other AOR bands that Alison would have taken me had we continued to share our evenings.

I had chosen a new path and was going to stick to it. I was becoming an indie kid.

— — — —

That night I wrote yet another long letter to Alison telling her about Richard's brush with the boobs and told how I was worried that he was so much more streetwise than I would ever be. Is confidence something you are born with, or can you get taught it? I pondered. Would I ever feel comfortable surrounded by half-naked women, or by Ahmet and Joe's porn collection? I asked Alison in my letter.

After it was posted, I realised that they probably weren't the best questions to ask an absent girlfriend. I clarified in my next letter that I was being rhetorical of course - I didn't want her thinking that I was spending my nights dreaming of the Raymond Revue Bar or the contents of the Men Onlys and Mayfairs I had in my collection. And I wasn't using those images as surrogate company either. I was yet to come across the expression, 'When you're at the bottom of a hole, stop digging'. I wish I had - it was the key theme of her reply. I had thought maybe she would have liked to have checked out Soho with me, if and when she ever came on a reunion visit to London. The tone of her letter meant that plan was scrapped before it was suggested.

My letter writing had been pretty consistent throughout my time in London. Generally I was writing something every day and after three days would post the latest collected works to Leeds, from the post office next to the tube station in Willesden Green. I noticed that Alison's return letters seemed to be coming less frequently. Most of them started, "I've got a

few minutes before I go out, so thought I would write to you."
Neither of us had access to phones, so we relied on the written
word and when I could afford it the odd bunch of flowers.

Alison's letters were not only getting shorter, but the refer-
ences to a law student called Kia were getting more frequent. A
few letters in she changed his name to Keir, having realised that
the fellow student wasn't named after a blend of fruit juices.
I doubted that anyone with that name would ever amount to
much, although he was obviously a love rival in the making.
I mean it's not like anyone called Keir would end up leading
the Labour party was it? Apart from that dude, Keir Hardie,
who set the thing up in the first place. Keir, Keir, Keir. All she
ever talked about was Keir. How great he was at debating, how
strongly he felt about politics, how good-looking and funny he
was and how he would probably end up being Prime Minister,
or at least Leader of the Opposition. Bloody Keir, I was sick of
hearing about him. Keir in his checked shirts and floppy hair.
Anyone would think she fancied him.

Richard and I were lying on our beds, writing our letters
home to families and girlfriends, when he announced, "Oh
by the way, did I tell you that Harriet is coming down at the
weekend?"

I asked which weekend. He replied, "This weekend, as in the
day after tomorrow."

Harriet was a smiley bubbly brunette who was in the year
below us at school. She was still there, doing her final year of A
Levels. It was the one good thing about Richard – he had stuck
with her exclusively for the last two years and they really looked
solid, even though they had many miles and life experiences
between them.

Harriet had the kudos among her mates of having an older

boyfriend in London. It also helped her cred that she was an occasional singer in 'Fungus the Bungus', the other school band that my brother Daniel played guitar in. Her voice was like her - small and it wasn't up to much - she used to use two mics to make herself heard.

Richard and Harriet were a bit of a golden couple and it seemed that the 100 plus miles between them wasn't a big deal. They'd continue to make sweet music together.

Richard was prone to flamboyant gestures. The year before, he took her to Paris for Valentine's Day, which had been mid-week so they both had to skive off school. As Richard is half French, this was home turf and gave him even more opportunity to impress. His forthcoming French degree at Uni was kind of an obvious choice. He was already fluent and it wouldn't involve much work. Typical Richard.

Because neither of their parents would sanction overnight stays in the same bed, Richard would book a room in the hotel next door to our school. They'd both tell their parents that they were somewhere else, my house being his usual fake destination, and slope off to the hotel, for what I can only assume was a night of 'sexy time'.

Our school operated a two-bell system. One bell would sound at the end of a lesson and one five minutes later for the start of the next. It was to give pupils the time to get between rooms. Because the bells were on a basic alarm clock programme, they would also sound twice at the start of school. One would go off five minutes before school was due to start and the second, five minutes later, when we were supposed to be at our desks, ready for registration.

Richard had worked out that when they heard the first bell sound they would have just enough time to get out of bed, get dressed and make it into school for the first lesson. He used to laugh how we would all be trudging past the hotel window whilst him and Harriet would be eating croissants in bed watching us.

Talk about getting your money's worth. There were days he would arrive in class still putting on his tie and with his shoes and flies undone. We all knew where he'd been the night before. Lucky bastard! He never told us how he funded those hotel rooms either. He didn't have a part-time job like the rest of us, so I can only assume some Richard-style skulduggery was in play. He did confess towards the end of the year that they had once 'done a runner' from the hotel and that the owner was in his garden the next day trying to spot which of the 800 boys owed him the price of his room.

Fortunately for Richard, we all looked pretty much the same and at least 10 lads were pulled over and pinned against the wall by the red-faced manager. The common room was full of stories about how each boy had been beaten up by a random bloke in the road, with each tale being more outrageous than the last. I knew the truth and enjoyed listening to the bullshit some of the hard lads who wanted to kill us were coming out with. I was surprised that they weren't crying to their mummies about the nasty landlord.

Richard looked round the wardrobe at me. "Well? Are you going to say anything?"

I wasn't sure what he was driving at.

"Harriet hasn't visited since I moved in here with you. We'll have a lot of catching up to do." I was still none the wiser, or maybe nun the naive.

"So I can't have you snoring in the corner when she's here can I? As I said, we've got a lot of catching up to do. You'll have

179

to move out for a couple of nights."

Eh? Two nights from the day after tomorrow? Where to exactly?

"You've got mates. Ask them if you can stay with them." He was referring to Judy, the friend studying at Westfield College. I told him that was ridiculous on so many levels.

"Ask the guys at your workplace, one of them is bound to offer you somewhere to crash on their floor. You can use my sleeping bag if you want. Anyway, from what you've said, you'll probably get an offer of sharing a bed with one of them and you won't need my bag."

This was actually a bit shit. He wanted me to ask people I barely knew if I could stay over at theirs, so that he could spend a weekend in bed with his girlfriend. OK I had no plans to be an audience, but couldn't Richard make other arrangements and slope off with Harriet somewhere else?

"Dude, you know the price of hotels, you fucking work in one. I can't afford to go somewhere else with Harriet. She will be here at the weekend and I hope you won't be. Sorry. Let me correct that. She will be here at the weekend and you won't be."

He had a fair point and I guessed that this would then mean that he owed me a favour. Although thinking about it, he already owed me a pile of those.

I went into the hotel the next day and asked Ahmet and then Joe if I could crash at theirs for the weekend. Ahmet declined on the basis of the 'baby being a problem', which I think was code for 'my life, my house, and my wife aren't as glamorous as I've told you' and he wanted to maintain the mystery of the Ekmekci story. Joe just laughed.

"What Marco, you want to stay at my place? Sorry my friend.

If you want that sort of thing ask Andrew, Didier or Karl." I don't think he quite understood what I was asking him.

Jean-Mick was on the late shift so our paths crossed for a couple of hours in the afternoon. I found him in the office cleaning glasses.

The request was put to him and I was pleased to see one of his broad smiles flash back at me.

"Yes, why not? I will have to ask Simon to stay away. He is my roommate. You know him, he works in the store downstairs. He has friends and family all over London, so for him is not a problem."

I did indeed know Simon. He was the oriental-looking guy in the basement storeroom, who wore a black suit and one of those cravat-type ties to work. That always struck me as strange, as the only people he saw all day were the waiters and housekeepers. I had never had a conversation with him other than to put my order in and sign the paperwork on my way out.

I now felt really guilty. Simon would have to leave his bed in order to make room for me, so that I could leave my bed to make room in Richard's bed for Harriet. But Jean-Mick told me it wouldn't be a problem, so that was good enough for me.

— — — —

About that time, I had started to 'collect' small soap bars from the guest bathrooms. This was a pragmatic solution to a practical problem. I needed to wash at home and therefore needed soap. The hotel had a lot of soap and if they preferred my armpits to be fragrant, then it only seemed right that they should help me to achieve that.

The little wrapped bars were put out as part of the complimentary toiletries in every room. I figured that if the guest hadn't used them they were fair game. The guest could have just as easily taken them home with them when checking out, as I did at the end of the day. In other words, I was helping myself in rooms where the guest had recently left and before the maid had got in to restock the bathroom. It was a victimless crime, although I realised that collecting soap would be seen as strange by most people and I suspect is still regarded as bizarre today.

I was at this point taking maybe five or six bars a day. I had a hole in one of my coat pockets, so the soap would fall into the lining. Security never seemed bothered about bag checks anyway, and if they were to do that, all they would find would be my Walkman and Filofax and the occasional contribution from Joe and Ahmet's porn mag mountain. Look in my pockets and you'll find nothing in there. Just don't frisk me or ask what the little lumps were that inhabited the bottom hemline of my coat.

Richard thought the idea was hysterical. "If you are going to nick something, get something worthwhile like booze or bathrobes, or something we can give to our families as Christmas presents!" All of his suggestions had value in cash terms and the hotel would no doubt miss them. I didn't like the idea of stealing stuff other than the 'free' bars of soap. We got paid so little anyway that stealing items of value from our employers would mean that they would have even less to pay us with. Anyhow, how would I get a bathrobe past the security check point?

So the weekend duly arrived and I took Richard's sleeping bag with me into work. I had turned it inside out and hung it out of the window the day before in an attempt to fumigate the sack. That didn't work, so the blue man-made fibres now smelt even worse, as I had added to the memory of Richard's sweaty nights with his Lynx Amber body spray. It would have to do.

Jean-Mick was on a day off, but had given me his address. He lived in Warwick Avenue.

I trudged on to the Bakerloo and emerged in a very posh part of town. Tall white stucco buildings from the turn of the century lined the tree-filled boulevards. There was even a canal running alongside Jean-Mick's road with barges and houseboats moored to the towpath. It was all very lah-de-dah.

I rang Jean-Mick's doorbell and the amiable Frenchman let me in. It was the first time I had seen him out of uniform. He was dressed head to toe in Kappa sports gear.

"Marcoose! Come in." We walked into his rented room at the back of the house, one wall was just a collection of panes of glass. This must have been a conservatory in years gone by. I 'wow'ed' appropriately and told J-M that it was a lot bigger than the hole I had found myself in North West London.

"I like it." Jean-Mick said. "The room is cold in winter, but when summer arrives, it will feel like Cannes."

The room sported the usual bedsit collection of wardrobe, table, chair and two single beds. J-M and Simon didn't have the luxury of our L-shape layout back in Willesden, so they really did lack any privacy - just two beds against two walls with about ten feet in between them. I thought, maybe the French don't care about seeing each other's bodies.

"Take a seat Marcoose." Jean-Mick said pulling out a cork from a bottle of red wine and whipping out a cheeseboard from under a Mayfair magazine on his bed.

I plonked myself down on Simon's bed with a mouthful of

Brie and a large glass of wine.

"Salut!"

I took a sip from the wine glass and looked round the room. Next to the marble fireplace was a pile of porn mags about two and a half feet high. J-M saw me looking at them. "Not all the treasure gets taken by the pirates," he pronounced.

It looked as if he had been top slicing the magazine business Joe and Ahmet were running. They wouldn't be happy if they found out. I asked how he was doing it. "Some come home from the rooms and some come home from the office," he said.

I hadn't taken J-M as a purveyor of porn mags, but he was definitely one hell of a collector, if not just a real perve. Maybe he was just French and liked looking at semi-naked women.

Next to the pile of magazines were around 50 beige linen napkins randomly arranged. I'd seen some of these on Floor Service trays. Beyond those, around 15 to 20 folded white hotel towels. Two bathrobes that would normally be in one of our suites hung on the back of his door. What the hell?

"Those are from Simon." Jean-Mick explained. "He likes to be clean."

So do I, but who needs that many napkins and towels? What about the wine? "Stolen." And the cheese? "Stolen." Anything else? Jean-Mick leaned over and picked up his coat which was hiding something in the corner of the room. It was covering one of our mini-bars. "We have no fridge, so this was a good idea. If you want a strong drink later, the fridge is filled every day. We call our room the 7th floor."

"Quel voleur!", I declared. I still remembered a few choice French O level expressions. "Vous etes les coupables!" J-M was impressed that I could accuse him of thieving and being guilty in his mother tongue. I wonder why those sayings had sunk in.

This was theft on a wholesale level. I could only think that Simon's role as the mild-mannered stores manager allowed him access to whatever came into hotel and he was siphoning off linen, towels and other food items. But how was he covering his tracks? This was more than Ahmet and Joe's breakage box.

"Simon works in the ideal department for him. He likes to take souvenirs home. He doesn't sell them, he just keeps them. Some of them we can eat and drink." I pointed to the mini-bar.

"He got that when the hotel started the department. Some fridges were broken when they arrived. They were returned, mostly. This one had just had a hole on the door. Simon brought it home as a souvenir."

And the contents?

"Simon is the Store Manager. Et voila!"

It seemed that the mild-mannered Simon was feeding the two of them from the kitchen supplies and providing all manner of items, including the sheets I slept in for the next two nights. It went some way to explaining how they could afford to rent a room in such a nice part of town – it was probably the only thing the two of them ever spent a penny on, unless he had stolen that too.

Six months later Jean-Mick and I would be sat drinking beers in Cannes. I reminded him about the two nights I stayed with him, this time using my O Level French. Jean-Mick gave me one of his wide smiles. "After you left the hotel, he was arrested. I think he was sent to prison for a month" I hope the two of them didn't think I had reported him after my stay, as I hadn't. The fact that J-M had invited me down to his home town to live the life of the jet-set playboy with him (on 10 Francs a day – roughly a pound) suggested he knew it wasn't me.

Mind you, I was tempted. Mini-bars hated Floor Service and Floor Service hated mini-bars. We both hated the Staff, Security and Accounts Departments more. Lucky for Simon, no one actually gave a shit about Stores, which is probably how he was getting away with it in plain sight.

I suspect Simon is now an international jewel thief, or maybe working in some other hotel elsewhere in the world still pilfering the odd wedge of Brie, or bar of soap as a souvenir.

Week 6

Richard seemed happy enough when I got back to the room after my stay with Ali Baba and the one thief. He had just got back from taking Harriet to Paddington. He looked suitably shagged.

"Hey, I had a good idea yesterday for sausages." I feared his was one of his more bizarre sexual perversions that I really didn't want to know about. That seemed to be confirmed when he added, "I did it with Harriet yesterday and it worked really well." I was totally confused.

He retrieved a half-open pack of actual pork sausages that had been on the windowsill outside. We hadn't got around to nicking a fridge yet like Simon and J-M and the cold of the winter was our icebox.

"Look and learn, my friend. Look and learn."

"I think you mean watch and learn, my friend. Look and Learn is that boring comic that the nerdy kids read when we were in junior school."

He gave me a blank look in reply. He wasn't a nerd and, unlike me, was allowed proper comics as a kid, some with actual cartoons in them.

Richard put two sausages into the groove of the adapted wire coat hanger that we used for making toast and clipped it on to the front of the electric bar heater. He was right, within a couple of minutes they were sizzling nicely and a few minutes more they were dripping fat on to the carpet and were ready to eat.

"Genius or what? Toast, tea and now sausages, what more could you want?" Maybe cheese, wine, smoked salmon and caviar, but I thought I'd keep quiet about that even to him.

The sausage dinner kept us going for three nights more. On the fourth night I got home to find Richard eating a jam sandwich. I asked whether I should crank up the sausage machine?

"Ann came up earlier. She said she could smell cooking coming from our room yesterday and she checked it today when we were both at work. She went a bit mental about the fat mountain on the carpet in front of the sausage machine. She said it was a fire hazard and that whatever we were doing we had to stop. She asked me what the sausage/toast rack was for. I told her you were into art and were making sculptures out of coat hangers as your psychiatrist had told you it would be good as part of your 'treatment'. Good job she didn't look out of the window at the new pack of sausages that's out there."

We had been rumbled. No more electric bar cooking for us - and no more sculptural therapy, not that I needed that - yet another Richard fiction. From now on it was going to be purely cold food at home, with the occasional Pot Noodle and as many hot meals as we could stomach at work.

Richard jumped off his bed. "You know what? It seems like a major bummer not to eat the remains of our larder. They cost me money and I'm not going to let good sausages go to waste. There are starving children in Africa who would love these. By the way you owe me 40p for your half."

"Turn the fire onto four bars and we will have a last blow-out. Can you eat six of these beauties?", he said holding up the value pack of processed meat he'd got from the corner shop on the way back from Kilburn tube.

Soon we were batch processing sausages. Four at a time. We'd just finished cooking the last batch when there was a knock at the door. "Marcus, David. Open up." You know that time that I felt my balls shrivel up? It happened again.

Richard opened the door before I had a chance to hide the sausages, which I now held behind my back. The hot fat was oozing through their skins, burning my hand.

Ann walked in purposefully. "I can smell cooking. Are you cooking David? I told you that you can't cook in here. Why are you still cooking?"

Richard reassured her. "I think you can smell the kebabs that Marcus brought back from the station. They smell really bad, don't you agree? I have to sleep in here and he'll be farting that smell all night."

She pointed at the fire, which still had the wire sausage-holding device clipped to it, along with the addition of a fat drip tray made out of the card back of an A4 note pad. How would we explain that?

By now the sausages were giving me third degree burns behind my back. I told Ann that it was one of my art projects, that must have fallen off the mantelpiece. Unlikely, but at least it echoed what Richard had told her earlier. I really did not want to lie to her. She was an honest and caring woman. She deserved more.

Richard added, "There seemed to be some sort of deposit in the carpet in front of the fire, so we thought we would soak it up with that piece of cardboard. Look, it seems to be working, there's fat all over it." Ann failed to notice the fat was on the upper side and not the side touching the carpet.

She gave us a look of 'I know you are up to something, so whatever it is don't do it again' and left us to carry on not doing it.

I threw the sausages on to a plate. Ouch, they really had burnt me. I told Richard, no more cooking, it just wasn't worth it. We settled down to watch some TV and write a letter home, me with blisters starting to form on my fingers.

Once that was done, I picked up the copy of the Evening Standard lying on the floor. Flicking through it, there was a small story about something called the Terry Higgins Trust, that had been set up in honour of a man who had died from a killer illness that was being caught by gay men in America. It seemed pretty irrelevant in the overall scheme of things. I wondered if Andrew knew any Americans.

————

Back at the hotel the following day, Joe pulled Andrew, Didier and I aside to tell us about a conversation he had had with the Hotel Manager – someone I was yet to see let alone meet.

"I'm going to say this to John tomorrow too. I was with the top guy talking in the foyer this morning. He said that the Mini-Bar department are a bunch of scruffy looking dickheads who are dragging the reputation of the hotel down. He said I was OK and Ahmet too, but the rest of you have to sharpen up. Try getting a shave for a start Didier, and Marco, what's with the dirty shirts? You smell like one of the Porters."

I tried to tell him the shirt had been washed last week, but he shut me down. Joe was really mad.

We all felt uncomfortable with the dressing down.

"Andrew, why the fuck are you still wearing your restaurant waiter jacket? We wear burgundy in this department, not white. Go to Mr P and get a spare Floor Service jacket off him when we're finished."

"So there is some good news. The top guy says the four of you can go for a fitting at the hotel suit maker, and get some brand new jackets. We'll do that next week."

I was impressed. Not only were we going to get new uniform, but it was going to be a fitted suit to boot. The closest I'd been to a tailor was watching Dennis Taylor play snooker on TV.

Andrew was dispatched, having finally accepted that he had to give up the white Nehru collared uniform worn by the Commies downstairs. He was going to come back as a new Capitalist pig.

"Eh. Mr P told me he only had one spare. This one." Andrew was no more that 5 foot 6 and the jacket he now had on, whilst being the right colour, looked like a hand-me-down from one of the Harlem Globetrotters. It was not only XXLarge but XXLong. His hands were hidden inside the sleeves, and the bottom of the jacket, which was supposed to sit on his hips, was down to his knees. I thought he could have put one of the fridges in with him and quite happily done up the buttons.

"What the fuck Andrew?" Joe exclaimed. "Were you listen-ing to me? The big manager thinks you are a bunch of scruffy arseholes. If he sees you in this he'll think you're taking the piss out of him. Come here and let me roll up the sleeves so you can get back out there and do your fucking job. How do you think you're going to open doors if your hands are missing?"

It was generally accepted that it was OK to mercilessly mock the penguin. Laughing at him, rather than sympathising with any predicament he found himself in, seemed to be the group think and Joe was the ringleader. I wondered if it had been any of the rest of us, Joe would have been so cruel. It was obviously a joke that Mr P had decided to play on one of his Mini-Bar enemies and Joe had reinforced it. It seemed the boss of Mini-Bars hated Floor Service, but hated one of his own team even more.

However, by the end of the week, Joe had magically got hold of a smaller jacket for Andrew, but not before he had to check a good couple of hundred rooms looking like he had shrunk in the bath.

———

The next day I came across a room on the 3rd floor that seemed entirely different than normal.

The whole room was covered in talcum powder. It looked like an explosion had happened at the Imperial Leather factory, or someone had been trying to stage a snow scene. That was odd for starters. For a moment I wondered if the white powder was something more powerful, but there was too much of it and the Floor Service guys would have relocated it back to their office by now if it was.

I could tell that the guests were still staying in the hotel as most of their possessions had also been thrown around the room. I felt sorry for the maid who would have clean and reset it for when they got back later.

I went across the room. Turned on the radio as usual and opened the fridge. More than half of the contents had gone. So I set about writing out the docket, before refuelling it.

I looked down. On top of the fridge were a bunch of Polaroid photos. It only took a moment to realise that they had been taken in the same room before the snow storm.

The photos featured a relatively large middle-aged woman in various states of undress, ending in a few of her naked, sprawled across the bed, leaning against the bathroom door frame and lying in the bath, which was dry. There were also a couple that had been taken in front of the full length mirror and featured, not only her, but the man she must have been with. I was shocked. This was the first time I had actually seen anyone having sex. All the mags we had in the collection were just pictures of naked women, and those were more artistic than biological.

I put the photos back on the fridge. Filled the bar and went back on my round.

Half way through the shift I needed some more clean glasses, so went back to the office. Joe and Ahmet were chewing the fat with J-M who had just arrived to start his late shift. I told the three of them what I had seen down on the third floor and commented that I really had now seen everything. And I meant everything.

The three of them looked at each other and charged from the office onto the fire escape with me closely behind. The glasses would have to wait.

Joe knocked the door of the Polaroid room. No answer, so the four of us headed in. The maid hadn't got to the room yet, so the talc explosion was still on display. "Looks like someone had some fun", Ahmet commented.

We walked over to the far corner of the room and the three of them started to study the artistic merits of the Polaroids, passing them around between them, commenting on the various poses and positions, as if they were judging Crufts.

The general view seemed to be 10 out of 10 for effort, but 4 out of 10 for style.

Suddenly the door clicked and in walked the middle-aged couple we were looking at in the photos. Only this time they were fully dressed. Before they had realised there were four men in burgundy jackets stood in the corner of their room, Joe quickly placed the photos back on the fridge.

"Can I help you?" said the male guest in a heavy German accent.

Joe turned to the fridge and slapped the side of it hard. "Now Marco, I think that should mend it. Did the three of you see what I did?" Ahmet and J-M both spontaneously stroked their chins as if they had just had an educational revelation. Joe turned to the guests.

"Sorry Sir, we were just fixing your mini-bar. Have a nice day", and with that the bar fixing brigade trooped out past the confused couple.

It was probably at that moment that I realised that most electrical items can be fixed with a good slap and that the average human body is not a thing of beauty. Clothes are one of our better inventions.

Week 7

W hat was it with naked people and this hotel? I'd heard a few moans and groans whilst doing the late shift, coming through doors that really should have been thicker. I was tempted to knock on the door and shout 'mini-bars', completely ignoring the Do Not Disturb sign. I wondered what, or who, lay beyond. The one time I did intrude on a couple who frankly should have made more noise to warn me about what they were doing was a little embarrassing for all concerned.

Me, "I've come to check your mini-bar Sir".

Him (wearing only a towel), "Have you? Why don't you just fuck off instead".

Me, "Shall I come back later?"

Him (agitated, to me), "No. Just fuck off."

Her (from somewhere inside the room), "Who is it?"

Him (to her), "Some twat."

Me, "I'll just fuck off".

No tip there then.

One morning, I was doing the usual checks. At room 211 I knocked, listened, announced myself and entered what I expected to be an empty room. As I turned on the radio I looked up, and sat next to the window was an attractive young blond couple having their breakfast. I apologised for not noticing they were there. I then realised that they were very much there, and also totally naked.

"Carry on" the man said, as he continued to butter toast while the woman sipped her tea. I felt my face flushing and stammered something along the lines of how I'd be more than happy to come back later.

"It's fine. Do what you need to do", the woman added with an air of supreme confidence. To do what I needed to do, I had to squeeze past her to get to the fridge in the corner. I felt the arm of my suit jacket brush against her shoulder. It was a sensation that could best be described as erotic fear.

I knelt down to the bar and her torso was now in my eye-line. Do not look, do not look. I said to myself. I opened the bar. Nothing had been taken. But I looked. I hope she didn't notice.

For a fleeting moment I wondered if this was another honey trap laid on to catch corrupt staff members. But two of them, totally starkers? These people were taking their jobs as security guards way too seriously.

I thanked them and started to sidle past the table. "No, I want to thank *you*" she said, touching my arm as I passed by her. "Before you go, is there anything else you want to ask us?" he added. My rational mind had been scrambled like the eggs on the breakfast tray, so I could only blurt out, "Have a nice day!"

Had I just been propositioned? Was he expecting me to say, 'Er, yes, can I have sex with your wife?' What if I'd said that, even as a joke, and he had said yes. Worse still, imagine if I had said it as a joke and he hadn't thought it funny.

I reported the tale back to Ahmet later that day, asking him for his advice and wondering whether I did the right thing? Ahmet was philosophical about this one.

"You say they were both blond and had good bodies right? They hadn't touched the bar, but they wanted you to check it anyway. They were drinking tea and eating toast without jam or Marmite. The eggs were untouched. She touched your arm, but didn't grip it nor did she pull you towards her. He didn't look like he had a hard-on, although you reckon you didn't look to find out."

I confirmed that those were the actual facts of the case.

"I'd say they were definitely not Security. So they must have been guests."

Well that was worth it, thanks for that incisive analysis Ahmet.

"Oh yeah, I've just looked them up on the room database. They're Swedes. Those guys do everything naked. So I'm afraid to say, little boy, that they were just having their breakfast and not looking for a sex slave for the day. If you want to be one of those, I know a randy couple in Romford who would like to meet you."

Was this Ahmet bullshit again? I was disturbed for the rest of that day, not by the fact that I had been manhandled by a naked Swedish women, nor the fact that I had even thought that they could be propositioning me, but the fact that Ahmet said he knew a couple in Romford who would like me to be their sex slave. My God, he wasn't talking about himself and his wife was he?

Like everything else in the hotel, I put it down to experience and thought, one day I might write a book about this. About how I crammed a whole life's learning into a couple of months.

— — — —

I got home to find Richard slightly perplexed. He had been caught fare dodging at Kilburn on his way home. It transpired he wasn't bothering with the single-between stations scam any longer and had been just walking through the ticket line for the last couple of weeks.

"I'm afraid it's not the best of news for you Marcus. I gave them your name and this address." I was rightly pissed off. "I wanted to tell you so it doesn't come as a surprise. I hope that's OK and we won't have an atmosphere tonight." No, no atmosphere tonight, that would be coming tomorrow. Tonight I was just going to be extremely angry.

Apparently it was a spur of the moment thing on Richard's part. So I should expect a fine for fare dodging. The irony was not wasted on me. It was Richard who had come up with the one stop single/Central zone weekly pass concept, which saved us about £3.50 a week. I was really annoyed that he had got caught and framed me. Me, who at least paid *part* of my fare every day. True, I was only paying part of the fare, so maybe I wasn't that much better than him. Technically I was riding two stops from Kilburn to Finchley Road at the edge of Zone 1 for free. But I wouldn't have told a ticket inspector that my name was Richard. That was just fucking stupid!

The letter from London Underground arrived a couple of days later. Funny how quick they could be when it came to debt collection. I had the option of appealing. So I did.

I replied that whoever had used my name and address was unknown to me, but that I was not the person. If they looked at their CCTV, they would see a guy with curly dark hair, as opposed to my straight brown hair. My eyes are blue, his are brown. Ah. Hold on, I wasn't supposed to know who was impersonating me.

I redrafted it, attached a spare photo-booth picture and asked them to compare that to the culprit. Of course, I could be sending someone else's photo to cover my tracks, but for a £50 fine, this seemed to be too complicated, surely.

A couple of weeks later I got the notification that I was in the clear, but that I shouldn't do it again. What kind of a message was that!? I knew for sure whose details I would give if ever I got caught fare dodging on the tubes. Vengeance would be mine.

————

I found myself having to write a letter to Barclaycard too. I was in HMV and decided that I really needed a couple more tapes. My card was declined as I had maxed it out. Strange, I thought as I've definitely not spent £100 on music recently. Must have been a glitch.

When the next bill came, I had indeed spent £100, in fact a lot more. And I hadn't bought any tapes, but I had bought a load of bedding and clothes in Brent Cross Shopping Centre. I didn't even have a clue where that was.

For a day I assumed I was going mad. Had I had an episode where I'd blacked out and gone shopping, spent loads of money on credit and then thrown away all of my purchases? It was the only logical explanation, other than Richard had done the same thing having taken the card from my wallet. That seemed much more likely.

I confronted him with the bill. Not guilty, his verdict and he was personally affronted that I would think that of him. Given his recent track record, I could have expected a lot worse. He almost said as much when he declared that if he was going to steal my card it wouldn't be to buy pillows, even though I knew for a fact that he had a liking for softer ones than Ann had supplied us with.

I called the Barclaycard number on the bill and explained that something strange must have happened here. I was asked for the expiry date on my card. I read it out, it was the month before. The voice on the phone said that they had issued a new one. Did I have it? No. Could I put this in writing and they would look into it.

They wrote back to me roughly at the same time as the verdict from the Underground landed too. I had spent a couple of weeks worrying about £150 that I was going to have to find for a fictional fair dodge and an equally fictional shopping trip.

Like the Underground, Barclaycard told me I was in the clear. They had indeed issued a new card, but it seemed that never reached me. Whoever had opened the letter with it in must have taken the card and gone up to Brent Cross, which it transpired, was the closest large shopping centre to Willesden Green. Next time they would not send a new card to a shared property, but would forward it to a different home or work address. The implication of this was that someone in the house must have opened it in the hall.

Who did I know who would need a overabundance of bedding? Thinking about it, the pillows did feel a bit more comfy than before and I'm sure that I didn't recognise the sheets on the bed. Ann changed them once a week for us, otherwise we would be lying on the same ones as the day we moved in. And I doubt that either of us would have thought to wash them.

Surely my landlady hadn't taken my credit card on a shopping trip? In my new London life, anything seemed possible. No, not her. I concluded there was a baddie in one of the other rooms of the house. Probably the same person who liked smashing up bathroom suites, although in my mind Mr Ann was still in the frame for that one.

——— —

Mini-bars continued to be filled and I was now fully into the daily and weekly cycles of my working life. My eyes continued to be opened, but I had reached a point where I no longer got embarrassed, and at times I wasn't even shocked.

One early afternoon I walked into a darkened guest room, turned the radio on, pulled back the curtains and opened the mini-bar only for a groan to come from the bed. The guest was not only in the room, but he was in bed and asleep.

I offered my profuse apologies and started to close the curtains. By now the Japanese fellow had sat on the edge of his bed, fortunately in his striped pajamas. He was groggy, probably jet-lagged. I continued to apologise and started to make my way out of the room. He shouted, "WAIT!" after me. I thought here we go, he's going to take my name and report me for waking him up (I hadn't turned the radio off in my attempt to escape). He beckoned me to come back to him and reached into a bag on his bedside table.

"Take", he said putting a £50 note in my hand and rolling back over into bed.

I told him I couldn't. He didn't need to tip me. I hadn't done anything for him, other than acted as an early alarm clock. By now he had shut his eyes and was waving at me in a dismissive hand gesture trying to get me to leave him alone. I said again that I couldn't take his money.

"You take and GO", he commanded.

I'd been used to the odd tip provided through the Ahmet and Joe profit sharing scheme, but those were counted in the pennies rather than pounds. Not only had I never seen a £50 note in real life before, but I certainly had never held one.

A moral quandary was posed. Maybe I should just take the cash. The guest obviously either had a lot of it, or didn't know the value. Maybe he thought me waking him up for no reason was worth £50 of his money. The other option was to wake him up again and give it back to him. What if I woke him up again and he gave me another £50? What would I then do with £100 of trouble? Double or quits?

So I decided to put the money quietly on top of the mini-bar in the hope that it would still be there when he woke up. I turned off his radio and closed his curtains as by now he was snoring.

As I left the room, I picked up the Do Not Disturb sign hanging on the back of his door and switched it to the outside. Hopefully that would be enough to stop a Floor Service waiter from making the same mistake I did, and more importantly, save the old chap £100s in tips. Floor Service wouldn't be as scrupulous.

Yes. Despite a few weeks of having my moral compass severely compromised, I finally did the right thing.

Week 8

I confirmed my degree course for the following autumn. I'd decided not to go back to school to retake physics and chemistry A levels. There was no guarantee that another year would improve my grades and that I'd even pass physics this time, so I applied to some polytechnics. Bristol and Manchester wanted resits, despite three of my A levels being graded at two Bs and an E, but Oxford took me based on my application. Maybe they liked the cut of my jib or something.

It had been great to go to the campus open day knowing I had the unconditional offer. I felt very smug talking to other applicants over lunch, who were all comparing what grades they needed and discussing how their A Levels were going. Me? I'm on a year out, I've already got a place. Yeah, working in London and going travelling in the summer. Super superior. How cool am I?

I would be going off to do a BSc in Human Biology – one of only two places in the country that ran that course. My old Biology teacher at school had sent me the A Level Human Biology syllabus that a couple of other schools did. I looked at it and thought it looked very easy, only an idiot would struggle with the biochemistry sections. (By the time I finished at Oxford Poly, I would have managed to scrape a 2.2 in my BSc

Joint Honours in Biology and Psychology. I had struggled with biochemistry in my first year and was forced to change disciplines, mainly from being too cocky).

So when people at the hotel asked me if I was going to go to university, I could quite honestly put my hand on my heart and say no. I've got a place at poly - you know, it's like an A Level college that does degrees. It's where the thick people like me go to waste time before working in record shops. Sweet.

Having now sorted something for the following three years, it made me think about what to do with the rest of my 'gap year', rather the rest of my life. Apart from Richard, all my mates from home had gone straight off to start their degrees. They had all achieved better grades than me as a result of working harder, having bigger brains, or spending less time in the pub.

We were getting close to Christmas. I asked Richard about his plans and whether he'd given any thought to how long he wanted to stay in London and what about the rest of the year.

"Christmas... Well if you're going home then I might get Harriet down here and we can celebrate together." I doubted she would want to do that, despite his confidence that she would.

"Rest of the year. Not planning to be in London much after Christmas. I'm thinking of maybe going to India, or Bali. I quite fancy Thailand too and Australia."

They must be giving flights away for free, or he was plotting to bump off a relative and pick up an inheritance.

I suggested that his level of global ambition might need to reflect the amount of cash in his pocket. 10 out of 10 for optimism though.

Jean-Mick was planning to go back to Cannes. He had to do his National Service the following year and had already got a job lined up in the Carlton Hotel up for the summer. He had already booked a holiday in Florida and then a trip to Biarritz for some surfing. When J-M invited me to go down to Cannes and see what the French Riviera had to offer I jumped at it. This was my post-Christmas plan. I told Richard that he could go on his fantasy world tour, but I would be on the Cote d'Azur.

"Sounds good to me. When are we going?" Richard replied. So we had an escape plan. I wouldn't be able to shake him off just yet and sometimes, as the saying goes, better the devil you know. His command of the French language would buy him a ticket on my trip.

All we had to do was find a good date for both of us to quit our London jobs and get down to the South of France. Jean-Mick had already told me that he would be there from 1 May. It would be an ideal time as the weather would be getting warm, the tourists didn't start showing up until the end of June and the French weren't on holiday until August. We should be able to find a short-term flat to let in the 'off' season for very little money. Which, after all, was the best description of our collective budget.

It was something to look forward to. If we could survive this London experience I was sure that we would continue to thrive in France, despite my limited grasp of the language. Of course, for Richard it would be easy, given that his Dad was from Paris and he had been brought up bi-lingual. Why make life difficult for yourself?

———

We had a plan for the future, but had the day to day to deal with first. A late shift on a Saturday brought me all manner of hassle thanks to the Australian rugby team.

I was hoping to have a quiet evening cleaning glasses, listening to Capital Radio and seeing if any food had been left lying about on Floor Service trays outside rooms, when I got a call from the ground floor.

"Hello Reception here. There are 12 rooms about to check out in the next 15 minutes that will need bars checked. Can you ask the team to go to the following..." and a list was read to me.

Team? Team? The team was a team of one! By the time I got down to their floor, I'd have less than a minute per bar to make the usual checks. Just about doable if they hadn't been touched, especially as the rooms were all next to each other.

So I grabbed a pad of dockets and went down the fire escape two steps at a time to the second floor.

This block party booking had all raided their bars on an industrial scale. I didn't understand it. They must have hammered them that evening, as the bars would have been refilled by the day shift earlier in the day. A couple of rooms had piles of empty lager cans stacked in them too. The beer wasn't one we stocked in the hotel, so these guests really had come prepared.

In the history of Mini-Bars, this was wholesale bar carnage. It was the equivalent of the Battle of Waterloo, only the battle was taking place over just 15 minutes and the only casualties were empty bottles of booze strewn across bedroom floors. I was hoping for Blucher to come riding over the hill with his Prussian reinforcements, but no, I was left to fight this battle alone.

I scribbled away at each bar, writing out dockets as fast as I could realising that I wasn't going to make my deadline.

I phoned Reception from the 5th of the 12 rooms to explain the predicament and to list the items that the guests had taken so far. The call itself ate up the rest of my allocated checking time. The Receptionist at the other end of the phone got agitated, the guests were catching a flight and their coach was outside ready to leave.

I could hear the Head Receptionist in the background say to one of the guests, "We are so sorry that our Mini-Bar attendant hasn't been able to check all of your bars. Will it be OK to send you an invoice for the outstanding amount?"

I knew that Reception absolutely hated doing this as it meant loads of admin and invariably complaints from Accounts when the bills were not settled by absentee guests. In the hotel, Accounts would kick Reception. Reception would kick Joe. Joe would kick us and as we had no one else to kick, we would just have to try to make sure we caught late and early check-outs the best we could.

Joe knew it was impossible at times, so his kickings were more playful than full-on violent. However, he did take a lot of shit for us. It was a valuable lesson in how to be a manager and one I would take into my later career. Only kick those who deserve it and be willing to take a kicking for the team even when you are not at fault. How to Build Respect 1.01.

So I knew I had failed to meet my challenge. Now that the party had gone, the pressure was off and I could do the rest of the checks at a fairly leisurely pace. Radio on, fridge open, docket written, check the room for anything interesting I could repatriate back to the office, look for unopened soap, move on.

At the end of my shift I bumped into the Receptionist I'd been talking to. I vaguely knew him as a result of previous painful experiences. I asked about the late check-outs and whether we would be likely to get the money back. Who were those people anyway? They had destroyed the bars and downed an off-licence worth of lagers too.

"That was the Australian Rugby Team. Not the players. They stayed somewhere else. That was just the officials. They played this afternoon at Twickenham and by the size of the bar bill, they must have won."

I thought blimey, that was the oil capacity of the guys holding the magic sponges and the men responsible for rubbing Deep Heat into the legs of a bunch of meathead rugby players. I wonder how big the players' bar bill would have been?

Given that I have never really had much interest in rugby, I didn't even mention the story to Richard when I got in. Had it been the Australian football team, that would have been a different proposition. Although having said that, the Socceroos weren't exactly known for their prowess on the football field. They'd been at the World Cup once in 1974 and if I remembered rightly, were totally useless. I suspected that the football team's bar bill budget would probably amount to a couple of mineral waters and a bag of nuts.

The next day in the office, there was a lot of excitement. Apparently Ray Davies of The Kinks, and The Pretenders' Chrissie Hynde had stayed in the hotel the night before. Were they a couple? Seemed unlikely to me. Pity they hadn't wanted their mini-bar refilled. I tried to point out that the real excitement was the Aussie rugby team support staff having a massive binge session from our fridges, but the idea of The Kinks and Pretenders sharing a room and throwing TVs out of the 6th floor window was the subject of the day.

— — — —

Joe and Ahmet were pleased to announce that the new uniforms had arrived, with not a mustard yellow football/rugby shirt in sight. If we were to continue to be thought of as the 'those Scruffy Bastards in Mini-Bars', it would be down to our inability to master personal grooming. I was still shaving with Bic razors and hadn't managed to get to a barber, so I would probably be the one most likely to get a bollocking if the team was pulled up again.

We took the new trousers and jackets from the zip up bags and tried them on.

The fitting had been quite an experience. A proper gentleman's outfitter, in the middle of Mayfair, who had measured all the necessary dimensions, even breathing on the tape measure before taking the inside leg. Which I was told later was to warm up the metal tip of his tape.

He even asked us which way we 'dressed'. This caused much hilarity when Didier was asked. "In the bedroom", he had replied. When I was asked the same question, I had to confess to not really noticing before. I guessed my 'straightness' must be different from most blokes. Either that or my trouser snake was too much of a trouser worm.

So now we all had new burgundy jackets that fitted and a pair of black trousers that not only reached our shoes, but didn't sag on the bottom and would stay up even without a heavy-duty plastic belt. Each jacket had 'Mini-Bars' embroidered on the pocket. 'Jeeves of Mayfair', read the label inside. We were well chuffed. We had actual tailored jackets that fitted like gloves, rather than the mittens we used to wear that must have been found on a charity shop bargain rail.

Although not all of us were happy about our new costumes.

Andrew walked in halfway through the fashion show. "Eh,

where's my suit Joe?" Joe looked around him. "Not here, Andrew. How come? Did you go to the tailor to get the fitting?"

"When was that? Did you all go?" We all nodded. There hadn't actually been a set appointment, we were just told to turn up at the shop on the other side of Grosvenor Square at some point on a particular day. Andrew must have known about it.

"I didn't know when my appointment was. I was waiting to be given a time." Ahmet explained there weren't any. Everyone else had just showed up on the day. Didier even came in on his day off.

Joe leaned back in his chair. "Now we have a problem Andrew. Mr P wants his jackets back. I was only borrowing them off Floor Service for you guys, until we got our new uniform. Leave it with me and I will see what I can do." He wasn't happy and I felt sorry for Andrew. Of course it would be him that had mucked it all up. Just another reason for Joe to be annoyed with the penguin.

Joe disappeared with three of our old jackets. Ten minutes later he came back holding just one. "Andrew. Mr P says he needs yours back, but he gave me one to replace it with."

Andrew took off his jacket to reveal a pair of yellow braces underneath. He lobbed it across the room to Joe, who caught it with one hand and threw the other piece of clothing back to Andrew at the same time. The trade was done.

Andrew's face dropped. "Eh. Sorry Joe, is this the only one he had?" We all noticed the rolled up sleeve as he put his arm into it and it quickly dawned on us that Joe had returned with the oversized jacket that he'd made Andrew wear once before.

I suspect that he did it partly because Andrew was a no show at the tailors and he wanted to punish him. Or perhaps he thought Andrew wasn't to be trusted and he wanted to make a point about who was boss. Or it may have just been so he could invent a new nickname for his reluctant member of staff.

"Hey Marco, have you seen the Incredible Shrinking Penguin?" Joe thought that was probably about the funniest thing anyone had ever said.

— — — —

On my way home that evening, I thought what the hell. After Tron I'd promised myself never to go to a cinema on my own again, but the guys in the office had been discussing Mad Max, in between taking the piss out of Andrew. It sounded great. A film about an angry policeman. Well maybe not *that* great.

The film was on at a small cinema next to Kilburn tube and I had just enough money for a ticket.

The cinema was pokey, the screen not quite flat and the sound awful. Twice the film jammed and the house lights came on before the cinematographer got the reels moving again.

I hadn't expected the dialogue to be in a foreign language, Australian. It reminded me of the night before, and failing to check those rugby officials' bars in time. Halfway through the film, I realised that was the reason that the guys had been talking about Mad Max in the office. It must have been the Aussie connection and I'd subliminally absorbed the instruction to continue my relationship with the land down under. If they had been talking about Fosters or Castlemaine XXXX, maybe I'd be sat in a Aussie bar now instead.

But it was indeed a bloody great movie and one that I would keep harking back to when I was at home down the pub with friends from school.

"Have you seen Mad Max, the version originale?" (It was later overdubbed with American voices, as Mel Gibson's voice was impossible for the Yanks to comprehend.)

"I saw it one evening in Kilburn after my shift at the hotel. Did I tell you that I was working in London, learning valuable life-skills, whilst you were at uni listening to some overpaid boffin droning on about ox-bow lakes in your lecture theatre?"

Yes, Marcus, you fucking did tell me a million fucking times, now fuck off!

Week 9

I had a visit from my Dad. My real Dad, not Richard pretending to be half of my parents. Which is ironic as my Dad was also a Richard. Confusing eh?

I'd not seen Mum and Dad since moving down to London, thanks to our crazy shift pattern. It didn't give me enough time to get the train home and back again, without making it a pointless trip.

I'd booked Christmas off, even though the hotel was expecting to be at near capacity. The French guys weren't going back to France, and as for Andrew, who knew where he went after leaving the building. So at least I'd get a Christmas dinner and the chance to stick cigars in the pockets of all my old mates down the pub.

I was in the office when the phone rang. It was the friendly receptionist from the night of the Australian beer monsters. "Hi Marcus, your father is down here."

I thought, bloody Richard. How am I going to explain how my Dad is actually the same age that he looks - 18. As I was six months older than him, he'd had me before he was born. He hadn't thought about that one had he?

So I angrily got into the lift and stomped into the hallowed ground of the front lobby. I went over to Gaston, the Head

Receptionist to ask where my 'Dad' had gone.

"You are not supposed to come into the Foyer. Only Reception, Concierge and Management are allowed in here. I will have to ask you to leave." He pointed to the far side of the Reception space to a man sitting on a long sofa. There indeed was my Dad.

"Hello Marcus. I was in London on a business trip and thought I would pop in to see you. Have you got time for a coffee?"

I was a bit annoyed with him. Partly because of the ticking off from Gaston about coming into the Foyer even though I knew I was banned, and partly because it was obvious that Dad hadn't understood that I was working. I told him I didn't think I could join him for coffee, I had fridges to check. I'd actually finished checking for the day, so tried not to look like I was lying.

"Don't you get breaks? Maybe we could go in the Grosvenor Bar over there. I could do with a sandwich or something. What do they sell?" I told him I had only been in there once before to get some glasses when we were short one time. I wasn't familiar with the menu.

"Well perhaps now is the time to find out." Dad picked up his battered black briefcase and took a couple of steps towards the archway with the red and black 'Grosvenor Bar' sign over it. *(Years later, that sign would become a feature in our garden bar at home. Good old eBay!).*

I didn't move. I told him I appreciated that he had popped in, but I really was in the middle of a shift and my boss would be wondering where I had got to. Also I wasn't allowed in Reception, so the longer we stood here talking the more trouble I was going to be in. Sadly, he and I hadn't had much of a relationship for the best part of ten years, including all of my teens, and the idea of having a one-to-one conversation with him would have made me squirm at the best of times.

Dad told me he understood that I had to work to the rules and that he, Mum and my brothers enjoyed reading my letters and were looking forward to seeing me at Christmas. He then put a £10 note in my hand, "Here have this, it would have been spent on lunch."

Later that day, when no one else was in the office, I phoned Hammersmith Odeon's box office to see if they still had any U2 War Tour concert tickets. They had one left, right at the very back of the upper gallery. I booked it.

With the rest of the ten quid I bought four cans of Castlemaine on the way back home. Richard and I drank them in record time that night. Cheers Dad. I may have been a 'See You Next Tuesday' to you that day, even to the point that I was embarrassed that you turned up at my workplace and people saw you. I'm sorry I felt like that.

You just wanted to be the kind of dad that most people had and I was mean, but I did get to my first-ever London concert thanks to your unexpected visit and the money you left me. Whilst I don't think young Richard ever said thank you to me for his share of the beers, I would like to say thanks on his behalf.

————

In total contrast, the following day we had a departmental lecture from my surrogate father, Joe, about using toilets and radios. I was guilty of both. But I wasn't guilty of the third thing he warned us about.

The radio thing was just a habit. Every time I went in to check a room's bar, I'd lean over the bed to the radio switch and blast out Radio 1 from the speakers that were built into the headboard.

A standard mini-bar check could be achieved in about half a song. My U2 tickets were bought off the back of hearing 'Sunday Bloody Sunday' on a tinny hotel room radio and learning that the band was on tour. I'd already been a fan from school days. 'October' and 'Boy' were two LPs that Alison and I could agree on as being 'great albums'. Along with Shalamar's 'Friends', Fleetwood Mac's 'Rumours', the first Police LP and of course, Santana's 'Moonflower'. As mentioned earlier, my music taste had needed updating before I got to London. Thank the Lord for his master's voice.

Joe told us that the turning on the radio thing had to stop – it was annoying the maids apparently. Not because they didn't like music, but because they weren't allowed to listen to the radio when they were making up the rooms. They probably thought we were up our own arses at the best of times, without Radio 1 for company.

It soon became apparent that Joe was relaying a message from his harem, the Housekeepers. Normally he wouldn't take any interest in actually managing what we did on a day-to-day basis.

"The other thing, you've got to stop doing is using the toilets."

A collective question mark formed over us. Working conditions were bad, but not being able to go to the loo?

"No more pissing and crapping in the guest rooms. I know who is doing it. Housekeeping have told me. How the fuck do you think the guests like it when they arrive in their rooms to find Mini Bar skid-marks in their bogs?"

True I had never been to the staff toilets in the basement. What was the point when each room had a loo in it? It was just a waste of time going down there. At least I had enough common sense to only take a piss in the toilets that were yet to be cleaned by the maids. If the toilet had already been fouled by a guest then my additions wouldn't be noticed. Freshly prepared bathrooms were off limits in my mind. Surely the others didn't take a shit in clean toilets before the guests checked in? How stupid would that be.

The only exception was when we were up on the 6th floor in the office. The staff toilets were literally as far away from us as any other point in the hotel. Joe did allow us to pop into 624, a guest room next door, as long as we promised to flush it. We had to reserve any poo action for the toilets downstairs in the basement, or save it for our own, probably stolen, bog roll.

You may wonder why toilets were so important to this story. Hygiene factors had to be satisfied after all (and yes we always washed our hands, I think). A lot of this was about keeping the maids happy. And if the maids were happy, the Housekeepers were happy. And a happy Housekeeper would be more likely to want a word with Joe. Which made him very happy. And if Joe was very happy, he would leave us all alone.

Joe then turned to the third item on his team meeting agenda. His frown was an attempt to put on a serious face. Ahmet looked like he knew what was coming and started to laugh when Joe opened up with, "Finally I need to talk to you about being perverts".

— — — —

Christmas was rapidly approaching and I was wondering whether I really wanted to be in London for much longer. I mean, how could I go on working there without the toilets or radios? It was Alison's birthday in early January too. Missing that would be really difficult if I was in London, as she had already talked about having a party.

London was wearing thin. I was bored of being hungry and smelly and finding entertainment in doing daft things with Richard. Sometimes it felt like we shared a cell rather than a bedsit. The game of 'seeing who can throw a penny closest to a wall' does get a bit dull after playing it for three hours straight. Fortunately I had a scrabble set that kept us going for weeks. Our accumulated scores were in the tens of thousands by the time we left London.

One night, Richard invited me to go with him to Westfield College again, this time as he was going to be playing his collection of buskers' tunes in the Student Union Bar. He had asked his old rhythm guitarist from the school band to come along as well.

The guitarist was Nick, or 'Nicole' as we called him, given his surname was Coles. I hadn't realised that Nick was on a year out too and would end up at Oxford Poly alongside me. Well, more like at a long arm's distance for most of it.

Nick and I never really got on at school. He was just this Scottish introvert in a different form to us who happened to play a few chords on guitar. His school band, which also featured Richard, was called x-Alibi and were pretty incompetent musically. They wanted to be Steely Dan but lacked the talent and charisma. Or tunes.

At the first gig, Nicole played the whole set facing the back of the stage as he was so nervous. He had borrowed one of my brother's effects pedals. Daniel was in a band in the year below and was rivalling Richard for the award of the 'coolist kid with an axe' at school.

By the time the pedal was returned it was really knocked about and the battery was flat. Nick reckoned it had 'fallen out of the boot of a car'. So Daniel thought Nicole was a bit of a dick too and I went round to his house to tell him so. With hindsight, I may have just been jealous of Nick's friendship with Richard and my indignation about Daniel's fuzzbox was more than just defending the honour of my younger sibling.

So here I was with Judy, our friend from home and resident Westfield student, necking our snakebite and blacks, when the Student Union President walked in. He went over to where Richard and Nicole were setting up their gear and told them that they couldn't play as it was against SU policy to have musicians playing in the college who were not members of the Musicians' Union. The only exception were Westfield students. As Richard and Nicole were neither they had to pack up and go.

Talk about embarrassing. But at least it was good to see Judy and just about OK to see Nicole again.

The staff Christmas party was happening at the end of the following week and I decided to make that my last day at the hotel. I would have managed to last 10 weeks, which on the face of it was pretty pathetic, but was 10 weeks more than I had expected. The party could be my leaving drinks.

— — — —

Sorry, I may have forgotten to tell you the rest of the pervert story. Wouldn't want to leave you hanging. With or without a gimp suit on.

As I said, Joe had put on his most concerned frown and looked us each in the eye before announcing that he had to talk to us about being perverts.

There is always that thing when someone accuses you of something that you know that you are totally innocent of, but you feel guilty nevertheless. This was one of those moments. Without a shadow of a doubt, the four of us were thinking the same. Joe was about to reveal something that had lurked in the shadows about each of us, something we were not even aware of ourselves. He was about to tell us we were all perves and he had the evidence to prove it.

The word 'pervert' seemed to struggle to escape his Mediterranean mouth. It was almost as if by saying it, Joe thought he would turn into one himself. Now that the word was out of the bag, he only had two strikes left, before he would become the Pervert Man.

I wondered if J-M and Didier were, like me, expecting the next sentence to include the words 'Andrew', 'Arabs' and 'more than just a tip'. But sadly, none of those appeared. Only in Joe's nightmares maybe.

Joe went on.

"How many of you know Jimmy in the kitchen?" None of us admitted that we did. Being a mate of Jimmy's was obviously going to make us a pervert in Joe's eyes, so best not to acknowledge his existence. We had passed the first test.

"Jimmy is that little KP, the one with one leg shorter than the other. Are you sure that you don't know who I mean?" The two Frenchmen shrugged and Andrew shifted from one foot to the other, having found a fascinating patch of floor tile to stare at.

"Jimmy had his balls cut off by the Staff Department yester-

220

day and you won't see him again." I wondered what the porter had done to deserve this. Despite that threat being offered to me when I first started, I was yet to hear of anyone actually being castrated. I knew that the porters were also the bottom of the pond, so I was surprised to hear that one had even been noticed, let alone being sacked for gross misconduct.

Joe continued to tell us about poor little Jimmy, who it turned out couldn't say no.

"Jimmy Jimmy was found by one of the Housekeepers in a guest's room, with a pair of knickers over his head and his cock in his hand. He was giving it a good old tug in front of the full length mirror. It turns out that length was not proportional to height and the Housekeeper thought for a minute that he was a right charmer. Until she realised he was wearing the guests' knickers and what he was doing with his trouser snake."

We burst into a mixture of incredulity and hysterical laughter. Except for Andrew who looked as if he had sucked a lemon (with, or without teeth) and kept repeating a low 'no' over and over.

Perhaps he had known the small mummy's boy and did what he was told by him. But now Jimmy's gone. Probably in an ambulance, as the Housekeeper had delivered a knee between his legs when he turned round to show her what he was doing. Such a silly boy.

We all stopped thinking about how to apply Undertones' lyrics for a moment and Joe finished the story.

"Staff Department want to know how he got a room key. I told them not our fault. They also wanted to know if any of us had seen him in action before. He confessed that this is a regular hobby of his. I told him we hadn't - as I'm sure you would have told me." He was not wrong, this misconduct story would have been office gossip gold dust. Andrew looked even more shifty. Was he letting Jimmy in to rooms so that he could rifle the guests' knicker drawers?

"So anyway. I have to tell you all not to go through guests' drawers, or touch anything else belonging to them." It seemed a strange request for Joe to make. I had never thought of looking at their stuff before now. The idea just hadn't bubbled up to the surface. I suppose I was too busy nicking soap and looking for porn to fund Joe and Ahmet's side hustle.

But now, of course, he had not only put an image in our heads that we would never be able to forget, but planted an idea there too. So our new routine would be, turn on the radio on entering the room, have a piss on the way out and, in between, open the wardrobe to see if there was anything worth perving over.

Unless you have a fetish for men's pinstripe business suits, you would have been sorely disappointed.

Week 10

I was very sad to break the news that I would be leaving to the team, especially to Joe and Ahmet who I felt I had been in the trenches with and had got to know really well. I told them that I had had enough of London, and I needed to go back to some fresh air and get my head sorted out before my next big adventure, which was most definitely not going to be uni.

Joe almost had a tear in his eye when he decided to have an Audit Drinks party a couple of weeks early and we cracked open some fresh stock from the shelves. The remains of the bottle of Jack Daniels that Mohammed had tried to destroy a couple of weeks before was fished out from its hiding place. All this at 9 o'clock in the morning.

When Andrew came in to refill his trolley, Joe called across, "Hey ISP, good news and bad news. Good news - Marco is leaving. Bad news - you can have his jacket."

I knew the transfer of the uniform was good news for the team, in that Andrew would now be identifiable from the 'Mini-Bars' insignia on the top pocket, but still pretty much bad news for him, as I was nearly a foot taller than my little Freddie. He would still be an Incredible Shrinking Penguin.

One of my regrets about leaving was not having the chance to see him in my fitted jacket. I did ask J-M how Andrew had taken to wearing his new uniform, when we were sharing a crepe in Cannes one evening. J-M gave me a broad smile and said "Incroyable pingouin retrecissant." I didn't need a dictionary to know what that meant, or a photo to imagine him waddling down the corridors with my old jacket reaching down to his knees.

My last few shifts went off without any drama. I spent my last day off in HMV buying a couple more tapes and then heading up to find Judy at Westfield to see if she'd like to go to our Christmas party as my plus one. She wasn't there, but I left her a note and amazingly, she tracked Richard down at his hotel and got a message to me that was a 'yes, as long as you are not wearing that stupid hat'.

I had already knocked on Ann's door, earlier in the week, to explain that I was leaving London, but that David/Richard would be keeping the room on. He planned to move a mate from his own hotel to fill my bed, even though I was confident that he would never be able to find anyone to truly take my place.

Ann came to my door later that evening carrying a tray with some crisps in bowls, and a tumbler glass half full of whiskey.

"I thought you'd might like this" she said. It was a kind gesture. I thanked her profusely and asked her if she wanted to drink it with me. She declined. I apologised for all the messing about.

"Ah, it's not a problem. You two remind me of what my son was like at your age."

Before I shut the room door on her, I asked her where she was from, as I had never been able to work out her strong accent.

Ann laughed and threw her head back, "Kilburn, so it is. And before that Limerick, in Ireland."

So there I was thinking I was talking to a Russian, or maybe someone from Poland or Czechoslovakia, Romania or Bulgaria and all the time she was from just down the road.

My last shift went by in a blur, mainly because Joe decided that the fridges could be checked the following day as he, I and Ahmet had some serious farewell boozing to do before the staff Christmas party started. There was also a lot of man-hugging and a couple of tears too. Joe's parting gift was a box of hotel soaps signed by the team and all three housekeepers, who it turned out did have a soft spot for me even though I had been too scared to talk to any of them. How did Joe know about my soap collecting habit I wondered? I guessed that he probably knew what everybody was doing in that place, to whom, with whom and where. Joe really was Mr Jupiter Hotel.

That evening I met Judy by Bond Street tube. She was sober and I was already drunk from the excesses of the afternoon. I tried to explain how much I'd loved working there and how much I loved the people, and by the time we returned to the main doors, she had nearly talked me into asking for my job back. As this was party night, we could go through the front entrance. Look at us, all grown up.

The party was held in the ballroom on the lower ground floor, which was accessible though the foyer. I had never had any reason to go in there before. Which was ironic, as 33 years later I would make another visit to that space, dressed in a dinner suit for an awards event. As you can imagine, most of my conversation that night started, "Did you know that 33 years ago, I used to work here?" Nobody actually cared, although they were quite surprised that I could even remember that far back given the amount of booze I had consumed in the intervening period.

The ballroom was, and is, a hangar of a space. The hotel had decorated the room in suitable Christmas themed tat, even though it was still a month away. I suspected that the decoration was for the paying punters that the Banqueting people had in the diary in the lead up to Christmas. If anything we were just a practice run for the real parties that they were looking forward to hosting. Get this staff thing out of the way as quickly as possible guys.

We were allowed to take a glass of sparkling wine from a tray, which obviously would not have been champagne, and found our places at the tables. The hotel had decided to split teams up to try to break down some of the differences between departments. So none of my guys were on our table. That was probably a mistake, given how much hatred there was between different floors and factions, so by the end of the main course, people had drifted into their cliques. And most of those drifted away from the tables to the bar for more booze and fags.

There seemed to be a lot of familiar faces missing from the room and a lot of faces I hadn't seen before. I wasn't even sure at the beginning of the night that we had come to the right event. Of course, the hotel was still open so there was a skeleton staff working above us on the floors and some of the party goers would disappear between courses to start a shift, whilst others would literally take their place and pick up their knives and forks.

I could see that Judy was feeling uncomfortable and my own discomfort with this very odd party couldn't have helped. I was supposed to be the urbane man who could introduce her to the room and tell amusing anecdotes about each person we came across. As it was, all I could manage was to tell her that I didn't know who anyone was and the best policy was probably to get quietly pissed and eat the tasteless slabs of meat that had been presented to us.

At one point Floor Service Karl walked past the table wearing a deep purple paisley jacket - the only suit in the hall that, apart from mine, that wasn't black. I did the usual Karl-Judy, Judy-Karl thing. He said, "Yeah. Nice. I thought you had left?" and walked off.

A guy I'd met once from Concierge had a brief chat with me as I stood at the urinals. We talked about the other time we met, and he told me about a bunch of flowers....

I was just about to say to Judy that we really ought to go, mainly as I was getting to the point where my head was spinning and I knew it wouldn't end well, when Ahmet appeared. I asked him where everyone else was.

"Joe doesn't come to these, Andrew is on the late shift and John went home. He is coming back later with a couple of French girls he knows. Didier is on his day off." So much for the leaving drinks guys. Any hope of impressing my old friend from home with my new friends at the hotel had finally disappeared. I was Billy-No-Mates after all.

"Look Marco. I've got to get home too. I'm covering your shifts until we get a new guy, so need to get some sleep. Nice to meet you Jilly." He started to walk away but spun on his heel. "Oh yeah. I forgot to ask you, did you ever buy any crap from Joe?" I nodded and with that he was gone.

Judy and I left shortly afterwards. It was a pity, as I would have liked to have seen J-M turn up with a woman on each arm. I had no doubt they would be uber-sexy and dripping with French chic.

Judy and I had been friends at school mainly as she went out with one of my drinking mates and she knew Alison quite well. We hadn't really spent a great deal of time talking before and I couldn't tell what she was less impressed with: the food; the lack of people to converse with; the pay-bar; the fact I was drunk and she was sober; the lack of entertainment – they hadn't even booked a DJ; or the terrible light gray suit I had picked up from Mr Byrite for £39.99 earlier in the week.

I suspect that suit was the crowning glory on a fairly terrible night. That particular item of clothing was later to become my graduate job interview suit. No wonder I ended up working in a record shop. The unpopular hat disappeared at the first student event I went to at Oxford Poly - a Blues Brothers disco. Lost but not forgotten.

––––

The following day I packed up my new tape collection, which had had Public Image, B52s and Talking Heads added to it the day before and stuffed it with the rest of my dirty clothes, the hat and the Byrite suit, into a large green army kit-bag I had found in a luggage shop on Oxford Street. I contemplated whether to take any of Joe and Ahmet's pornshare collection home with me. I'd felt a degree of shame about having a few girlie mags in our shared room and I had never told Richard where I had hidden them. I suspected he had his own stash anyway.

Being more worried about the magazines being found by Ann in the room after I left, or even worse by Richard, I decided to take them with me. The idea was to put them into a rubbish bin at some point before I got home. Of course, each bin either had too many people near it or was too full, so I flitted from one bin to another, like a human fly, never finding one where I could offload my collection without having an overwhelming wave of embarrassed nausea.

When I got home, they were still in my bag and I would have to find a new hidey hole in my family bedroom. My clothes weren't the only dirty item to come home with me.

Before heading to Paddington, I stopped at a payphone to call Alison. She was back from Leeds for a couple of days.

I gave her the good news that I would be there by about 6 pm. Would she like to go to the pub for a long-awaited reunion?

She told me that she had a couple of university friends from Leeds visiting and it would be tricky and that she was heading back in the morning. She didn't tell me she was actually having a house party the following night with all the old gang, except me. I found out about it a couple of days later, when I was down the pub with Simon, my old mucker from school, who forgot he had been sworn to secrecy.

"Ali told us you were still in London and that you two had split up. She had a friend from Leeds there. I think he was called Kia. Seemed like a nice enough bloke. Confident. Sort of chap who could be running the country one day. I hate to tell you this Marcus, but it looked to me that he was well into Ali and she wasn't exactly pushing him away. I suppose there are plenty more fish in the sea."

Easy for Simon to say. Not so easy for me to hear.

We had both moved on. She had spent a term being a student and finding new fun. I'd spent the same time learning about life and feeling generally miserable. I had missed her too much and it had pushed her away. Being 18 and running a long distance relationship without any way to communicate other than letter

229

writing was always going to be doomed.

I wrote to her to tell her that I knew about her secret house party and her special guest. It was over. I was full of indignation and misplaced anger for being taken for a mug. I didn't know if I was more frustrated with her for finishing our relationship that way, or for spinning a story to my mates about why I wasn't at her party. I was just an angry young prat - no wonder she had managed me out.

'Put it down to experience and move on' was easy to say and think. But our split hurt me deeply. It turned out that all those dreams we had were just a waste of time. If only I had been a bit more of a grown up, perhaps she wouldn't have had found comfort in the arms of that law student.

I was miserable, back home with months of boredom ahead of me. What would 1983 have in store for me I wondered. It couldn't get much worse than '82.

1983

I still had time to kill before going to polytechnic, not uni. Amazingly Alison and I got back together at the end of her Christmas holidays. It was that classic 'love will find a way' and we made it work for a while, if being a couple of hundred miles apart and seeing each other twice in four months could be called being back together.

There was always the spectre of Keir hanging over me and I was intensely jealous. I just didn't know if they were actually a clandestine couple and she was humouring me with her intermittent letters. She and I talked about going round Europe and working in bars over the summer, but that was just a dream that would have turned into a nightmare. We were becoming different people. She was a uni student having the time of her life and I was just a waste of space waiting for my life to start. Mine needed CPR.

Our relationship finally fizzled out when she told me that she was going to do some work for her aunt's house, back home in Gloucestershire, instead of coming on our European tour. Alison had obviously forgotten that she and I had been on holiday to her aunt's house the summer before...in Northern Spain. Maybe they had relocated, but I doubted it. So as an excuse for not going travelling with me, it ranked quite highly in the list of flimsies. I wondered where she was really going to be and with whom. This time I had to accept it was no longer any of my business.

So I farted about at home until Easter feeling sorry for myself. For those people who told me 'love will *still* find a way', I replied love had obviously got lost en route.

———

On 1 May Richard and I carried out our threat to hitchhike to the South of France, to continue where we left off in London. He had quit his hotel job a couple of weeks before and we were both ready for the sunshine to brighten up the wild and stupid times that we were bound to encounter. Jean-Mick had reassured us that an adventure was waiting in Cannes and we both needed to discover what it had in store.

By now we were both single and we were more than happy to have the sun instead of rain, and croissants instead of sausages. Our one bed rented flat in the 'Hotel des Sables d'Or' was a stone's throw from the beach and had a real kitchen, even if it was infested with cockroaches. Richard and I tossed a Franc and for once in my life I won. So I got the double bed and he had the uncomfortable fold up camper in the kitchen, which had to be pulled away from the walls at night to avoid our unwanted guests.

Our idea of getting a job was to get to work on our tans for two months by lying on the beach. We were planning to go back to England later in the summer and we wanted to take our bronzed bodies to the reunion parties that our school mates had planned. And what better way to impress the girls in the year below us, who we hoped would be letting their hair down post A level results.

We expected to be treated as A list celebrities on our return to the sleepy Cotswold villages, given the year we'd had. Yes, those tans would turn out to be relatively impressive and a ticket into most parties, even if mine was more fuchsia pink than Richard's chestnut brown by the time I got it home. I took a cautionary approach to tanning - avoiding the hottest part of the day, using sun cream (if I could scrounge it) and opting for a hat. Richard got roasted on day 1, but by the end of week 1 was able to go back out in the full sun with his skin now hardened off, having endured a few days of burning agony.

We still knew how to dilute Pernod, which was a ridiculously cheap way of sitting in a bar, and found entertainment in the smallest things such as the nightly sport of throwing orange peels through a neighbour's toilet window and waiting for the outraged, "Qui a lance des oranges!!" every morning at 8 am. Without the call of disgust from the orange peel-filled toilet, we'd probably have slept until mid-afternoon.

That acted as our daily alarm clock and got us down to the boulangerie then the beach, where we would hang out with a collection of continental drop outs, drifters, grifters and drug abusers for the next 10 hours. We even met an English guy who had been given a court martial from the French Foreign Legion the day before and was sleeping on the beach with literally just the clothes he stood up in as his worldly possessions. "It wasn't what I expected", was his reason for deserting.

A few weeks after arriving, when the money was getting really tight, we had managed to get a real job, washing up in a 'France Quick' in Nice, as our living expenses budget had dropped to roughly £1 a day. Get paid and eat cold burgers. Seemed like a good idea.

France Quick was/is a low rent version of McDonald's. Like most things we did, that job was flawed. The shifts ended at midnight, an hour after our last train back to Cannes. The only solution was to walk around Nice all night, then get the first train back in the morning at 6 am. By the time we got back to Cannes we would have less than four hours sleep, before we would need to be on the train back to Nice for the next 10-hour shift!

On the way back from Nice after that first shift, we fell asleep on the train only to wake up near Marseilles. The diversion knocked more than two hours off the available time to recharge our batteries. I quit before I went back to bed. Richard quit when he woke up, too late to go back to work.

Somewhere there is a French bank account with 180 Francs in it. My one day's pay (worth about £18 at the time). Eventually I will go back to Nice and buy that town.

The idea was to get UK dole money whilst we continued to 'look for work' in France. Although that hadn't turned out as planned, as the DHSS rightly said we were making ourselves unavailable to start work in England. We appealed their decision, saying we could get back in 24 hours of a job offer, but who was going to offer us work when we were lying on the beach in Cannes? The DHSS called that one correctly, even though we were stupidly outraged. How dare they stop our dole money! Anyone would think we were taking the piss.

Richard was once again caught fare dodging. He hadn't 'composted' his ticket on his way back to Nice to ask for his wages from our one night of work. But this time he gave the gendarmes his real details – intimidated by the size of their Alsatian dogs. So that fine took a big chunk out of our budget and we needed a way to make money that didn't involve any skill, nor a commute to any other city.

Richard was still trying to hustle whenever he could and I was happy to ride shotgun. At one point we had considered busking on the sea-front, by doing a dance routine to my Shalamar 'Friends' tape (a late HMV Oxford Street purchase, bought in memory of happier times with Alison).

Jean-Mick had lent us a ghetto blaster when we first pitched up in his town. It meant that we had the means to play a backing track, and we rehearsed the dance routine in our flat. It looked like a bastardised version of the Madness dance, that had been called 'the Biv' by our mates at school discos. Only Richard's band and so-called roadies were allowed to do the Biv - it was their secret handshake. If people like me tried to join in, we'd be told we weren't 'bivving properly' - not that there were any rules to it as far as I could see.

Jumping about at school parties was easy, but in Cannes there always seemed to be something stopping us from getting our Biv on.

The problem was that we needed to drink a lot of Pernod before we could summon up the courage to dance, and the drinking replaced the dancing. Our income from busking was negative. We had spent money on batteries for the cassette player and way too many Francs on Pernod. Our total time dancing was exactly 30 seconds, before we got too embarrassed, and during that 30 seconds not a single person walked past us. Dancing for money wasn't our thing.

Cross that one off the list.

Having no money did make drinking difficult, but that was helped by getting to know a couple of Norwegian teachers in the flat next door, who were more than happy to exchange their wine for our company for a couple of weeks. They loved French booze and we continued to help them to drink it. Night after night we waited for the knock on the door, before turning on the charm for a couple of hours, as thin-necked bottles of red wine disappeared and tales of hotel life were told in exchange.

We'd thought about selling stuff on the beach and made the mistake of asking in the Hotel de Ville, to be told it was illegal and came with heavy fines. That didn't seem to stop others from selling choconuts and drinks however. But Richard now had a criminal record from failing to buy a ticket on the train between Nice and Cannes, so it wasn't worth the risk. Leave that to the North Africans, we needed something a bit more English. Maybe we could start a fish and chip shop. That would go down well with the well-heeled millionaires who would be out for a stroll along the Promenade des Anglais every night. All we needed was a shop, a load of fish and some potatoes. And a deep fat fryer, and some basic knowledge of cooking. Newspapers to wrap the food in could be found in the bins. So that part was sorted.

Another fail. Actually, that one went on the 'fucking stupid idea' pile.

So we set up a shoeshine stall on the Promenade, only to realise that pretty much everyone was in flip-flops. If they had shoes on, they were white trainers. Not much call for black or brown shoe polish. That business flopped before it even started. Total number of customers on day one? Zero. Total amount of police hassle? A lot. Which was a shame as the Gendarmes were wearing the right kind of suitable shoes and we could have cleaned them.

We wondered what we could do with the brushes and polish we had bought and Richard asked in the Casino if we could relocate there. At least the staff wore shoes, so there was a chance of some business. Great idea - two sun-burnt English lads in luminous coloured surf shorts and t-shirts that had been worn for 20 days straight, cleaning shoes in the foyer for the well-heeled. Yeah, like that was ever going to happen. Although the Casino did pay us about half of what the equipment had cost us to take it off our hands, which felt like a victory of sorts.

Our conversation was reduced to two things. How we could make our budget of 10 Francs (£1) a day work and where was the cheapest place to eat and secondly, what we would do with any new found wealth once we managed to get jobs, including moving out of the cockroach hotel.

We took a week and knocked on every hotel and bar door in Cannes asking if they needed staff. My French and my confidence weren't really good enough for those interactions – but I thought I would be clever nevertheless and ask if they had any 'embouteillages', rather than 'travail'.

Jean-Mick had taken us to a party at an amazing millionaire-style villa in the hills of Antibes before he went to the USA on holiday. A French guy I met there had told me it was better to ask for 'job opportunities' instead of 'work'. It would be far more impressive to the bar managers and hotel personnel people to hear my command of the language if I went in and asked for the 'Bureau d'Embouteillages' - which he said loosely translated to the 'employment department'.

Of course, it was only when I got home to the UK that I found out I had been asking for the 'traffic jam office' for the best part of a week. No wonder most people I spoke to looked at me like I was from another planet, let alone England. The French were also going through a period where they were trying to strip English words like 'le pique-nique' and 'le weekend' from their language. A lot of bar owners in Cannes seemed to want to strip the English out of their town too. And who would blame them?

———

Jean-Mick had been right about what he promised me; we had everything we could have hoped for except work, food, alcohol and luck with the ladies... If I had been intimidated by the Housekeepers in London, I just wanted the ground to open up and swallow me whenever Richard suggested that we go over to 'say hello' to a couple of girls on the beach. I suspect we just looked like the couple of unemployed, skint, English dickheads we were. He'd saunter over and I would stay rooted to my spot on the sand, staring out to sea. Without fail, he would return alone shortly afterwards.

One night, towards the end of our stay, we did indeed manage to get drunk enough to talk to a couple of German girls in a bar. They spoke a bit of French, but neither knew much English. So we spent the evening trying to converse in French and what little German I could remember from school, 'Wo ist die bahnhof' etc. Luckily for them, they were leaving Cannes the next day, so they had the perfect excuse to decline our invitation to join us on the beach in the morning.

I did turn up at unannounced at one of their houses in Regensburg three years later during my post-degree travels and had the most brilliant hospitality from Andrea and her Bavarian boyfriend for the best part of a week. Hurrah for that evening trying to chat up a German in French and drinking enough of Cannes' Dutch courage to ask Andrea for her address. Watered down Pernod wasn't such a heinous crime after all.

It was a shame that Jean-Mick, the smiling Frenchman, disappeared for a month on holiday while we were there, as I suspect we would have met a lot more exotic people and maybe I would even have got a job sorting out traffic jams.

———

Cannes embraced us for two months, but we couldn't live on air and hope forever.

Richard and I hitch hiked back home over two days when our money ran out. Lucky for us, our first ride of the day took us all the way to Paris. Our driver was returning from selling some clothes at a market near Italy, or so he said.

It was nearly a ten hour drive in his Renault van. Initially we had asked for a lift to Lyon, as we thought he probably wouldn't want us sat next to him for more than 550 miles. When we got close to that city, Richard asked if we could stay on. The driver wasn't happy, but at least we did a good job of keeping him awake as we sped up the Autoroute.

When we got to Paris at 3 am, it seemed that we were going to be dropped off somewhere beyond the Periperique, well outside the centre of town. The driver suggested that we stayed in his spare room, which was on the ground floor of a shanty-type shack. The space was wall papered with hardcore porn photos and offered us just a small sofa by way of a bed. Richard and I got out shortly after the sun rose and before our guest had time to see if we were comfortable. In fact we hadn't slept, we were too worried that he was going to pay his wank palace a visit. The first metro train into the city was a welcomed sight.

We arrived in England with less than a Franc between us, as the price of the ferry crossing had gone up in the time we had been lying on the beach and we only just scraped the fare together. Had we not, we would have had to blag a seat in a cross-channel lorry's cab. Can you imagine that happening nowadays?

Richard and I did indeed make the most of that summer on our return. It became a blur of parties, booze and a series of short-term relationships, with girls who didn't mind my pink, peeling skin. But gradually he and I were drifting apart. We had been in each other's pockets for the best part of a year and the list of things that had annoyed me about him, and him about me, was getting longer. Twelve months ago I had found him funny, now I just found him bloody irritating.

Slowly we stopped checking to see if the other was going to be in the pub, or whether we may both be going to the same party and started to leave it to chance.

In the late summer, Richard and I went to a party in Surrey to visit two girls that we had met in the pub at home - they were staying nearby as they were competing in the Badminton Horse Trial, or looking after the horses, or something.

We thought we were on a promise, that never happened, so we went to the posh gathering and Richard caused all manner of friction with the local lads, who thought he was muscling in on their women. It was all very Neanderthal and for Richard and me it was our final hurrah. He took great delight in the atmosphere that we created by being there. On the other hand, I felt sorry for Saire, our hostess, who spent most of her night looking after her boyfriend who was crying his eyes out in the garden. I don't know what he thought we were planning to do. Apparently Saire's female friends (who all seemed to be about 15 years old and covered in pearls) were excited about meeting the two exotic boys from the country, but it all felt like a really bad episode of a teen drama to me. We were treated like a mixture of zoo animals and celebrities.

Richard took the train down to Brighton the next day, to sort out his digs ahead of starting at Sussex University. I took a train up to London to meet Saire's much older cousin who had been at the party. She had told me I had a very sexy voice, which she hadn't realised was due to shouting over music. I was bewitched when she gave me her business card and suggested I popped in to see her when I was next in town. I hadn't planned to meet her the next day, and didn't want to seem too keen, but hey.....she told me I had a sexy voice, apparently.

She hadn't told me at the party that she was gay. We had a drink in a Covent Garden pub and she casually let slip that of the six women that we were drinking with, she had enjoyed sex with four of them in the last couple of months. As predicted, I wasn't really equipped to reply to that. She was just way too glam for the likes of me. London had opened my eyes six months ago, but not that far. I'd got it completely wrong.....she had just liked my voice.

After that trip, Richard and I just stopped seeing each other around.

This was pre-internet and social media and once Richard had gone off to Brighton and me to Oxford, that was it. There was no way, nor reason, to stay in touch. So we just didn't bother. I carried on going to our local pub at Christmas, where the old gang would get together to compare student experiences. Later we would share stories of our new lives in the world of adulthood, but Richard never showed up. After a few years, I stopped showing up too. My life had changed and I was making new memories.

In the words of Talk Talk, I knew that 'The Party's Over'.

We had both put aside our foolish things and moved on.

12 months later.....

I was in London having come down from Oxford on the
Oxford Tube coach. A couple of student mates had asked
me to join them to go clubbing in Camden and later,
stay over at one of their parents' palatial houses overlooking
Regent's Park.

The coach stopped at Marble Arch before going on to Victoria
Station, so I hopped off and told them I would catch up with
them at Camden Palace later that evening.

Walking along Oxford Street was surreal. Many of the shops
had already changed in the last year. I was having to redraw
my mental map. A few of the old faves, like Selfridges, were
still there all lit up and inviting. I didn't point a camera at the
windows this time though.

At Selfridges I crossed the road and walked towards the hotel.
There it was, exactly as I had left it.

The man in the top hat had gone and had been replaced by
Steve, the bell-boy, who I had had the flowers incident with.
He opened the large glass front door for me. I smiled at him
like an old friend. He simply returned it with a half-hearted
effort. He didn't recognise me. I was just another punter who
needed the door opened.

I walked across the foyer. Most of the Receptionists were

new too, although one gave me a smile as if she knew who I was. OK, I wasn't completely forgotten. I was expecting to be challenged by one of the prowling concierge staff. No way was I going to be asked to leave the foyer this time.

The guest lift took me to the 6th floor. I turned right out of it, into a very familiar corridor. Nothing had changed, apart from a new fire door halfway down, which was pinned back ready for action.

I got to the Mini-Bar office and found two of the huge trolleys parked in the corridor. It was just like that first day on the job. I half expected to see Andrew peeping out from behind the shuttered box. I opened the door, thinking that I would walk into a room full of handshakes and hugs. I was returning to my guys, my team, my gang. I'm home, people and I've missed you all!

I took a couple of steps. Inside there were four people, arranged like the first morning I was there. Three on chairs, one perched on the desk.

The one on the desk looked up. "Can I help you?"

It wasn't Joe. And the other three were obviously not Jean-Mick, who I knew was back in France doing his national service, nor Didier, Andrew, nor Ahmet.

I explained I was looking for Joe and Ahmet. "Who?" the tall desk-sitter said. I told them that I used to work in Mini-Bars and asked what had happened to the old team. We were the original gangsters, we had set the thing up a couple of years ago. Where were they?

The three youths sat on the chairs remained mute. Their faces said it all, "Who the fuck are you?" They looked bored and, annoyingly, all of their uniforms were clean and fitted them. Not one needed a shave nor a haircut too. Come off it lads, we're the dirty boys of the hotel. What's happened?

The desk sitter replied, "I dunno. I think Joe got sacked. The rest of them left a long time ago before I started. There was a bloke who looked like the singer from Queen. I think he works as a commis-waiter in another hotel now."

There was a sum total of zero interest in knowing anything about the past team and what we had got up to. We had been the trailblazers, the guys who had made it all happen. Without our efforts there would have been no Mini-Bars department. These people owed us. They were our legacy. They could at least pretend to be interested.

I turned around with a tear in my eye. As I walked out I noticed that the porn mag pile had disappeared and Joe's breakages box was no longer where he had kept it. Progress, or had corporate hoteliers simply smartened up their act?

I went back to the guest lift, feeling very sad and sentimental for the times gone past, albeit just a year before. I wondered why the hotel had got rid of Joe. He was such a great manager and an even greater bloke. I had learned so much about life from him. He and Ahmet had opened my eyes wide during my time there and thanks to those two, I had a story for every occasion when out drinking with my student mates.

Walking back onto a gloomy Duke St, a red Ferrari zoomed past. I thought I saw Ahmet in the driving seat and Joe next to him, complete with knock-off Aviator sunglasses. Cool factor plus 10.

Maybe it wasn't my mates from the Mini-Bars, but to this day I want to believe that it was.

Playlist

E njoyed the book and want to hear the soundtrack? Here are some songs and bands mentioned in the story:

Part 1: School days

Santana - She's Not There

Led Zeppelin - Stairway to Heaven

Eric Clapton - Layla

Lynyrd Skynyrd - Freebird

Third World - Now That We've Found Love

Bob Marley - Jammin'

Abba - Waterloo

Donna Summer - I Feel Love

James Brown - Sex Machine

Yes - Going for the One

Rush - Spirit of Radio

Genesis - Follow You Follow Me

Fleetwood Mac - The Chain

Mike Oldfield - Tubular Bells (not all of it!)

Jimi Hendrix - Dolly Dagger

Black Sabbath - War Pigs

AC/DC - Touch Too Much

The Jam - Going Underground

Part 2: London

Steely Dan – Do It Again

Dubliners – Maids Never Wed an Old Man

Queen – We Are the Champions

Echo and the Bunnymen – Rescue

Ultravox – Vienna

Pretenders – Stop Your Sobbing

Kinks – Waterloo Sunset

Link Wray – Rumble

Teardrop Explodes – Reward

Simple Minds – I Travel

Siouxsie and the Banshees – Israel

Public Image Limited –Public Image

B52s – Rock Lobster

Joy Division – Love Will Tear Us Apart

New Order – Ceremony

Tears for Fears – Change

Billy Joel – Vienna

Bruce Springsteen – The River

Supertramp – Logical Song

Shalamar – Friends

Police – Roxanne

U2 – Sunday, Bloody Sunday

The Undertones – Jimmy Jimmy

Blues Brothers – Everybody

Talk Talk – The Party's Over

Guest Book

Feedback from visitors to **Hotel 1982**

"It's the fastest I've read a book in years. A pacy page turner. I really enjoyed it. I was actually surprised how much I did" - Daniel

"Thought it was well written, engaging and light hearted. It has no great moral message or meaning, but is a fun read and as good as anything else I've read recently" - Tom

"I couldn't put it down, even though my eyes were getting tired. I thought it was brill. I could smell the stench from you and Richard" - Melanie

"I've been laughing out loud at so many of the scenes that echo my experiences" - Jenny

"It really draws you in and you feel like like you are actually there" - Michele

"It wasn't as bad as I thought it was going to be" - Diane (wife)

"I'll read it when I've finished this one by Martin Heidegger" - Harry (son)

"You really think I'm going to read this?" - Millie (daughter)

Find out more at www.hotel1982.com

About the Author

Marcus Jamieson-Pond was born in 1963 in Cheltenham.

After moving to the Midlands, his family returned to Gloucestershire in his early teens. He spent the next few years looking
forward to a day when he would be able to escape from the
country.

His time in London was a stepping stone before studying at
Oxford (Poly).

Marcus now lives in Watford with his wife, children and
cat colony. As well as writing, and ghost-writing, he is a
professional photographer and acts as a corporate conscience
to businesses, having previously spent too long working in
glass and marble offices in the City of London.

email
  marcus@jampondphotography.com or
  contact@threeleggedstool.co.uk

You can connect with me on:
🜨 https://www.jampondphotography.com